SCHNIBBLES
times two
quilts from 5" or 10" squares

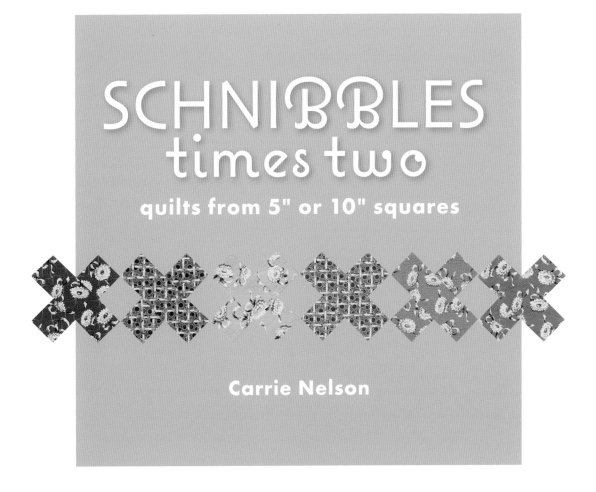

Carrie Nelson

Martingale®
& COMPANY

Schnibbles Times Two: Quilts From 5" or 10" Squares
© 2010 by Carrie Nelson

That Patchwork Place® is an imprint of
Martingale & Company®.

Martingale & Company
20205 144th Ave. NE
Woodinville, WA 98072-8478 USA
www.martingale-pub.com

Printed in China
15 14 13 12 11 10   8 7 6 5 4 3 2 1

**Library of Congress Cataloging-in-Publication Data
is available upon request.**

ISBN: 978-1-56477-986-1

Credits

President & CEO ▪ Tom Wierzbicki

Editor in Chief ▪ Mary V. Green

Managing Editor ▪ Tina Cook

Developmental Editor ▪ Karen Costello Soltys

Technical Editor ▪ Nancy Mahoney

Copy Editor ▪ Sheila Chapman Ryan

Design Director ▪ Stan Green

Production Manager ▪ Regina Girard

Illustrator ▪ Laurel Strand

Cover & Text Designer ▪ Shelly Garrison

Photographer ▪ Brent Kane

Mission Statement

Dedicated to providing quality
products and service to inspire creativity.

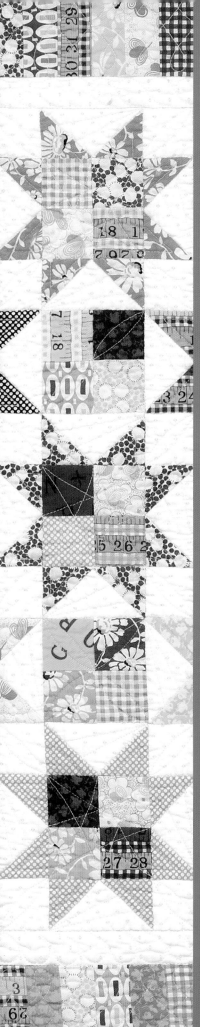

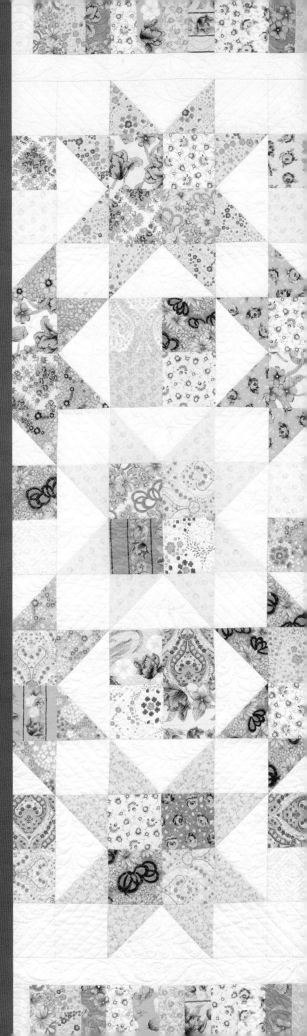

CONTENTS

PUZZLES, PESTS,
AND OTHER PROBABLY
NOT-SO-IMPORTANT STUFF ▪ 6

QUILTING CONFIDENTIAL:
HOW TO BAKE
A LAYER CAKE QUILT ▪ 8

THE PROJECTS

BENNINGTON ▪ 18

HOT CROSS ▪ 24

IMAGINE ▪ 30

LITTLE RED ▪ 36

MCGUFFEY ▪ 42

NICE DAY ▪ 48

OPEN SEASON ▪ 54

PLAN C ▪ 60

SCRATCH ▪ 66

SHORT STORY ▪ 72

SPIN CITY ▪ 80

X-RATED ▪ 88

ACKNOWLEDGMENTS ▪ 94

ABOUT ROSIE ▪ 95

PUZZLES, PESTS, AND OTHER PROBABLY NOT-SO-IMPORTANT STUFF

If you're reading this, I think it's safe to say that you already have an idea what this book is about—12 relatively simple, lap-sized quilts made with Layer Cake squares. But you may not know how this all came about: the Schnibbles, the little quilts, the big quilts, and the book. This section contains all the important stuff that you may—or may not—want to know before you start making any of the quilts, like just where that word "schnibbles" comes from and what it means, but I'll get to that in a moment.

Let me start by telling you that I'm always a little late to any party. It isn't that I'm trying to make a big entrance, it's that I can never decide what to wear, so I wind up being late no matter how good my intentions are to be there on time. And that seems to be a theme for many parts of my life; I've never been at the front of the pack when it comes to trends or hot new things. So when it came to the many wonderful precut fabrics available for quilters these days, it shouldn't come as a surprise that it took me a while to catch on.

When Charm Packs first debuted, I bought a couple. Okay, I bought more than a couple. They were hard to resist even though I didn't have any idea what to do with them, despite some well-intentioned pestering from a very nice lady named Lissa, the brilliant Director of Marketing for Moda Fabrics. In her quest to get me to use a few, she went so far as to suggest that I remake some of my existing quilts using Charm Packs. I have to tell you, that made absolutely no sense to me at all because that would mean using 10 or 12 Charm Packs—fat quarters were so much more efficient. I admit it took me a little while to realize she was suggesting that I make a small quilt. Except that isn't really my thing. But since I had all these Charm Packs piling up—Lissa's rather persistent that way—I sat down with ideas for making two small quilts.

One week later, I'd made six quilts. Another couple of days, and I'd made two more quilts. I'm wondering why nobody told me that small quilts could be so much fun!

It turned out that making a pretty little quilt was just half of the appeal for me. What I was really enjoying was what I can only call the "MacGyver" part of the process. I loved puzzling together what I could make while working within the four corners of those 5" squares and the assortment of fabrics in each pack.

Fast forward two years and 32 small quilts later; Lissa emails me about an idea she has using my little quilts

This is what temptation looks like. They're so irresistible! This is how I started using little bits of fabric to make little bits of quilts.

and Layer Cakes. Let me interject that after hearing her idea, I wish I could tell you that I had thought of it. It was brilliant. It was genius. It was—IS!—so stunningly simple that I found myself wondering why I hadn't thought of it! And, no, you don't need to answer that—I've already figured it out for myself. It has to do with that "genius" thing.

Lissa's idea was this: Instead of using 5" Charm Pack squares, use 10" Layer Cake squares, and resize the pieces and blocks accordingly. The big quilt would have the same number of pieces and blocks as the small quilt; the only thing different would be the size. How cool is that? She really does have good ideas, doesn't she?

There is one last thing to tell you before I get to all the really important stuff. It's about the word "schnibble." It is a real word and it's been published in the *Dictionary of American Regional English*. The first time I heard the word, it was used in conjunction with food and it was clear that it meant a small bite or a nibble. I loved the word and used it often, and when it came time to think of something to call my little quilts, I liked the idea of calling them "Schnibbles" for little bits. But having had a past experience with using words that didn't mean exactly what I thought they did, I did what any twenty-first-century girl would do—I searched Google for the word "schnibble" to see if it had any meanings that I really should be aware of beforehand. In one of those meant-to-be moments of serendipitous perfection, it turned out that this quirky little word actually means a scrap, small bits of cloth, or leftover bits of fabric.

And there you have it—using big bits of cloth and lap-sized quilts. No wonder I'm always a little late… it takes me a long time to get to the point!

Whoever said "less is more" never had a dessert. And she certainly never bought fabric!

QUILTING CONFIDENTIAL: HOW TO BAKE A LAYER CAKE QUILT

Think cake mix! Everything you need is in the box. All you have to do is pick the flavor that looks the most appealing.

Gathering the ingredients: Fabric Selection

The good news is you have to make only one choice: which Layer Cake do you want to use? The bad news is, do you know how many different Layer Cake collections there are to choose from? To make this easy, I just buy two each of the ones that I like and figure out which quilt to make later. And don't worry if you don't have two matching Layer Cakes, you can absolutely mix and match to get the number of squares you need. Really, as long as you've got enough squares, they can come from anywhere.

If you are short a few lights or darks, just add a fat quarter. With just a few exceptions, one fat quarter is equivalent to three Layer Cake squares. The only time this doesn't work is when you need all the pieces to be 9¼" squares or larger.

Mise en Place: Fabric Preparation

Mise en place (meeze on plahs) means to have on hand all the ingredients, already measured and prepared, so that you can cook efficiently and without interruption. We do the same thing with quilting, we just call it…what do we call it? Whatever, that's what we're going to do now.

When it comes to working with Layer Cakes and Charm Packs, there are a couple of things I think are important enough to mention.

What is a Layer Cake?

In quilting terms, a Layer Cake is what Moda Fabrics calls their packages of 42 precut 10" squares of fabric. Each Layer Cake represents a collection of Moda fabrics and contains at least one square of each fabric in the collection.

It's important for you to count the squares in your Layer Cake before you start because there have been some changes since Layer Cakes were first introduced. Early packages had just 40 squares, and even though the recent Layer Cakes have 42 squares, some of them have the old labels indicating that there are just 40 squares when there are actually 42 squares. (If you think that's confusing, try writing it!)

And so you know, a Charm Pack is a fabric collection of precut 5" squares. Older charm packs vary in how many squares they include, but Moda's newer collections will all have 42 squares.

Prewashing Fabrics

If you like to prewash your fabrics, you're going to have to get over that right here. It isn't possible. Well, it's possible, but it will create all sorts of problems so it's not worth it. I used to be a dedicated prewasher—that was the garment sewer in me. But I had to stop doing that several years ago because of time constraints. And when I started making quilts with Charm Packs and Layer Cakes, I couldn't worry about it, so I didn't. I do take a post-finishing precaution though: I always use a dye-catcher sheet when I'm washing my quilts for the first time. I wash my quilts in cold water using a gentle detergent, one that is free of fragrance, softeners, and other additives (something like Charlie's Soap or Orvus Paste).

This is what perfection looks like. You don't have to choose, because this isn't an "either/or" situation.
You can have both and you don't have to worry about what it will do to your hips!

Pressing Before You Cut

More good news! Unless you've been carting your Layer Cake or Charm Pack squares all over town, they probably aren't too wrinkled and shouldn't need more than a quick spiff-me-up pressing. But there is one important thing to mention—if you like to use steam to press while you're sewing, I recommend that you press the squares with steam before you start cutting. If the unwashed squares are going to shrink even a skosh from the steam, it's better that they shrink before you cut than afterward.

Which Way Does the Warp Go?

Warp is the lengthwise threads and weft is the crosswise threads. Since there isn't a selvage on the Layer Cake squares, there isn't a quick reference point to keep the direction straight. For the most part, it isn't going to matter which way you cut the pieces, but there are a couple of places where I think there is a

benefit to being able to cut strips on the lengthwise grain of the square, like for long strips and outer borders.

To find out which direction is which, pick up a Layer Cake square. Find a spot about 1" in from the pinked edge and gently pull the fabric in opposite directions. It will do one of three things—it will stretch a little bit, it will stretch a tiny bit, or it won't stretch at all. Whichever direction stretches the most is the crosswise grain of the fabric. The lengthwise grain, or warp, usually doesn't stretch at all.

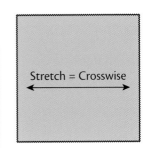

Cut on lengthwise grain.

You shouldn't have to test each square individually. When the Layer Cakes are cut at the factory, all the fabrics are stacked one on top of another with the selvages aligned. That means that all the squares have the crosswise and lengthwise threads going in the same direction.

Dessert Anyone?
How to Cut the Cake

I'm not going to pretend that I cut each and every square individually. No way! I'm going to stack those squares at least four layers high and cut away. In fact, you might want to stand back because I've got a sharp rotary cutter!

Seriously, I do cut four squares at a time but it isn't required. I want you to do what you're comfortable doing—whether that's cutting two squares or eight squares at a time. If you're new to cutting multiple layers, start with two layers and continue with that until you're comfortable with more. There are 12 quilts in this book so you'll have plenty of opportunities to work your way up to four squares.

Pinked Edges

When it comes to the pinked edges, this isn't a one-size-fits-all situation. There are places where I absolutely want you to remove the pinked edges and there are places where I want you to leave them as they are. After all, they're kind of cute.

When I first started planning these quilts, I purposely chose to size the pieces so that I could work with as many clean-cut edges as possible because I didn't want to have to worry about where on the pinked edge to line things up for an accurate seam allowance. So here's what you need to know about when to trim and when not to trim.

- If the cutting and piecing instructions don't mention the pinked edges, then you don't need to worry about them.

- If the instructions tell you to cut a whole Layer Cake or Charm Pack square in half diagonally, in half lengthwise, or in quarters, don't worry about the pinked edges. This will apply to squares cut for setting triangles, outer borders, and the blocks on one or two quilts.

- If the instructions tell you to "cut three strips" from the square and the length of the strip is the same size as the square, don't worry about the pinked edges on the ends of the strip. But the first cut you need to make before cutting the strips is to trim off one side of the square to give you a straight edge for your ruler. And make that first cut as tiny a sliver as possible; ⅛" or so is sufficient.

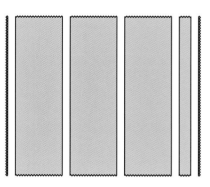

Tools of the Trade

No special rulers are required for cutting Layer Cake or Charm Pack squares, but listed below are a few that will make the job a little bit easier.

Layer Cakes:
- 9" x 9" or 9½" x 9½" ruler
- 6" x 12" or 6½" x 12½" ruler
- 6" x 6" or 6½" x 6½" ruler

Charm Packs:
- 6" x 12" or 6½" x 12½" ruler
- 6" x 6" or 6½" x 6½" ruler
- 4" x 8" ruler or 4½" x 4½" ruler

Putting it All Together: Piecing Techniques

This is the part where I tell you all of the things I may do differently than you would. I do what works best for me—these methods take into account all my bad habits and idiosyncrasies. You're not going to hurt my feelings if you prefer doing things differently. After all, you've got your own bad habits to work around.

Chain Piecing

Since all of the projects have multiple units or repeated units, chain piecing is absolutely recommended. Just feed each unit under the needle, one right after the other, without stopping or snipping the threads between the units. After you've pieced all the units, just snip the threads connecting the pieced units and press as directed. But if you sew like I do, I would suggest slowing down just a little bit between units as it helps you from having to rethread the machine every time the thread breaks.

Strip Piecing

Many of the projects in this book use pieces or units that can be strip pieced; that is, sewn together, and then cut into segments or pieced strips. But there are some projects where you will need to piece units individually. *Por quoi?* Because it will allow you to have a little more variety in the blocks, and since there aren't that many blocks, it isn't going to make a huge time difference.

Four-patch units. Sew two strips together along their long edges and press the seam allowances in one direction, usually toward the darker fabric. Cut the pieced strip into segments as specified in the project instructions. Then, using either matching or different segments, sew two segments together to make a four-patch unit; press.

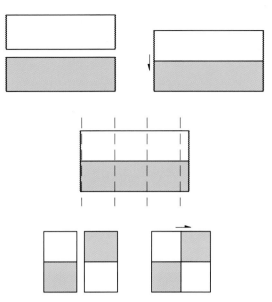

Making a four-patch unit

Piano-key borders. Join strips together in pairs and press the seam allowances before joining the pairs to make four-strip units. Then press the seam allowances before joining the four-strip units to make eight-strip units, press the seam allowances, and so on. The seam allowances can be pressed to one side or pressed open, although I prefer to press them open because it seems to reduce the bulk just a bit.

Pressing

I like to tease that I can make any block flat and square with enough heat and steam. While this is a little bit true, the reality is that you can make your quilting life a lot easier by how and when you press. So when it comes to pressing, this is what I'll tell you about my methods.

- Press early and press often. Even if it is just finger-pressing, I press every seam after it's sewn. And make sure that every seam is completely open when it's being pressed. That means that there shouldn't be a fold or pleat along the seam line on the right side of the fabric.

- To press the seam properly, I open the piece, right sides facing up, and lightly run my finger along the seam line to hold it open for just a moment before placing the iron on top of the seam to set it. There isn't any pushing of the fabric, especially at the seam line, or at least there shouldn't be.

• The demon steam—I wouldn't quilt without it! Some people think it's evil but I think it can be your very best friend. The key is learning how to work with it, or how to make it work for you. I don't think anything sets a seam the way a good shot of steam does. But pressing with steam can result in distorted pieces if you're not careful, or if your technique is a little more "ironing" than "pressing." When ironing you move the iron back and forth across the fabric, which can distort the seams. When pressing you hold the iron down on top of the pieces. And don't use steam on your pieced units if you didn't prep the Charm Pack or Layer Cake squares with steam before cutting.

Building Blocks: Making the Parts

Have you ever wondered why some recipes say "mix" and others say "stir"? What's the difference? This is the part where I'll let you know just how I'm going to "whip up" the parts that are going to make my quilt.

Triangle Units

A couple of the projects in this book use what is often called a connector corner or folded corner. A triangle-shaped corner is created by layering a square on top of a rectangle or larger square, right sides together, and then stitching diagonally across the top square. When making these units, I suggest the following steps.

1. Draw a diagonal line on the wrong side of the square, from corner to corner, using a permanent pen, pencil, or chalk marker. Or if you prefer, fold the square in half, wrong sides together, and carefully finger-crease the diagonal fold across the center of the square.

2. Place the marked square on a corner of a rectangle or square, right sides together, and carefully align the raw edges. Pin the marked square in place if needed.

3. Stitch along the line or crease, one thin thread's width from the line, on what will be the seam-allowance side of the line. By doing this, the triangle will result in a more accurate finished piece because you won't lose anything when the triangle folds over the seam allowance.

4. Before trimming, fold the triangle over until it meets the edges of the underlying rectangle or square and press it in place. Then fold back the top triangle and trim away both of the remaining excess triangles, leaving a ¼" seam allowance. I'm one of those folks who likes to trim both excess layers of fabric, but you certainly won't hurt my feelings if you prefer to trim away one layer of fabric only. And by pressing before trimming, I find that the pieces are usually square and accurate.

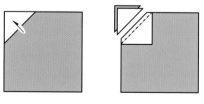

Flying-Geese Units

Here are the steps for my favorite, no-special-ruler-required method of making flying-geese units. For each set of four matching flying-geese units, you will need one large square and four matching small squares. The large square will become the large triangle in each unit and, for the projects in this book, will be 9¼" or 4¼" square. The four small squares will become the small side triangles in each unit, and these squares will be 4⅞" or 2⅜".

1. On the wrong side of each of the four small squares, draw a diagonal line from corner to corner using a permanent pen, pencil, or chalk marker.

2. With right sides together, place two marked squares on opposite corners of the large square. The points of the small squares will overlap just a little bit and the drawn line should extend across the large square from corner to corner, as shown.

3. Stitch a scant ¼" seam allowance on both sides of the drawn lines. Cut the square apart on the drawn line. Press the seam allowances toward the small triangles.

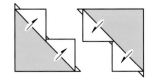

4. With right sides together, place the remaining marked squares on the corners of both pieces. The drawn line should extend from the point of the corner to the point between the two small triangles. Stitch a scant ¼" seam allowance on both sides of the drawn line. Cut the pieces apart on the drawn line. Press the seam allowances toward the small triangles.

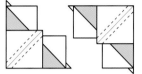

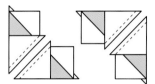

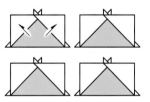

Assembling the Quilt Top

A design wall is everyone's first choice, but the floor or a bed will work for laying out your finished blocks. (It's a good thing my dog Rosie—more about her later—prefers the sofa, although she does love to stand in the middle of the bed if I'm trying to arrange my blocks there.)

I start by joining the blocks to make rows—horizontal or vertical, it doesn't really matter. Then I join the rows in pairs to make sections. Then the sections are joined to make halves, and so on until the center part of the quilt is complete.

Borders

Before I add borders to a quilt, I measure the length and the width of the quilt top in several places, but not along the edges because those can stretch a bit with all the handling. Now here's the part that confuses most of us—what do you do if the measurements aren't all the same? You flip the quilt over and see if there is something you can do to fix the problem. A couple of seams that are just a thread's width or two off of what they should be can quickly add up to ¼" or ½" difference in measurement. If the measurements are within ⅛" of each other, I don't worry about it obsessively. It's probably just a rumple in the fabric.

Cutting the Borders

I always cut the borders to size, except I also allow a little bit of leeway just in case I made a mistake. What that means is that I cut the borders a little longer than necessary but mark them to indicate the exact size they should be, which is dictated by the size of my quilt top. The measurements given in the instructions are for what the borders should measure if your quilt top is mathematically the correct size. These measurements are a guideline, and you should cut and mark your borders to the size required based on the measurements of your actual quilt top.

Inner Borders

Most inner borders are cut on the crosswise grain of the fabric, meaning that the border strips will have to be pieced together end to end to be long enough. I always piece these strips with a diagonal seam, as I think it makes the seam a little less noticeable. I also like to sew the strips together to make one really long strip, which is then cut to make the four lengths I need for the inner borders. Doing this distributes the seams randomly around the quilt, which helps make them a little less noticeable.

To piece the borders with a diagonal seam, lay one strip end on top of the end of the preceding strip, right sides together as shown. Stitch diagonally across the strips. Trim the seam allowances to ¼" and press them open.

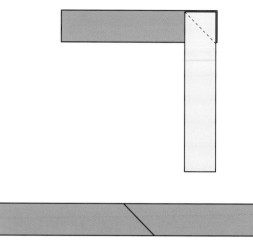

Outer Borders

I love pieced outer borders. Of the 24 quilts in this book, only four of them have a plain outer border, a ratio that generally holds when you include all the quilts I've ever made. I think there are two big reasons why so many of my quilts have pieced borders. First, I don't usually think of quilts as being made for a bed so I don't generally consider that when I'm planning a quilt. Or to put it another way, the finished quilts are the size they were meant to be. Too often borders look like they were added to make a quilt a specific size without consideration for balance or how well it finishes the quilt. Just as there are pictures whose focus is enhanced by a large mat and/or frame, there are pictures that are overwhelmed by anything bigger than a small, simple edging.

My second reason is a little harder to explain, so bear with me. It's essentially a proportional thing, and it depends on the color statement I'm trying to make with my fabrics. If any one piece of fabric or single color is of a greater amount in my quilt, the quilt is going to look to be that color. For example, if I put a red border on a scrap quilt that only has one or two tiny red pieces in the center of the quilt, most of us will see that quilt as a red one. But if I put a pieced border on the same quilt using fabrics from the quilt, no single color is dominant and the color statement of the quilt is made up of all the colors and fabrics in the quilt, as well as the blending of those colors and fabrics.

There are basically two different styles of pieced borders used for these quilts. The first border is made using strips that are pieced end to end to make a long strip. While these borders are pieced, the length is long enough that they can be marked and cut as though they were cut from a single piece of fabric.

Pinked Edges on the Borders

About those pinked edges—don't trim! Just use a generous ¼" seam allowance and lay out the rectangles so that the pinked edges all fall along the same edge of the border.

Once you've finished the quilt top and it's ready to be quilted, you can leave the pinked edges. Since you're going to need to straighten the edges after the quilting is completed, trimming off the pinking can wait until then. Why do the same job twice? If the edges and corners are straight and square enough for quilting, you're good to go. The pinked edges will be covered with binding anyway.

The second type of border is pieced to make a specific size—a border that has been mathematically calculated to be the same size as the quilt top. If the border you make isn't the size it should be or needs to be, don't worry! I have the technology to fix that! With a pieced border, you don't want to just cut it off to make it fit because it would probably look a little funny. Fortunately, resizing a pieced border is a pretty easy proposition.

To make the border a little bit larger, make several of the seam allowances a little bit smaller. Stitching the seam line just one or two thread's width inside the first line of just a single seam can increase the length of the border by as much as ⅛". And making a narrower seam allowance on three or four seams can increase the border length by as much as ½". The trick is to space out the seams you're redoing along the length of the border.

Narrower seam allowance

To make the border a little bit smaller, make several of the seams a little bit bigger. Stitching the seam line just one or two thread's width outside the first line of just a single seam can decrease the border length by as much as ⅛". And making a wider seam allowance on three or four seams can decrease the border length by as much as ½". As before, just remember to space out the seams you're redoing along the length of the border.

Wider seam allowance

The Final Finishing

Here are some pointers for turning a quilt top into a quilt and for adding the all-important label.

Batting

When it comes to batting, I do not play favorites. Just as colors, fabrics, and design can create a specific look or feel for a quilt, so too can the batting. I regularly use several different weights and types of cotton batting, and I also love wool batting. I've been using the awesome new 50/50 cotton/bamboo blend batting and it's terrific. I'm even experimenting with the new soy/cotton blend batting, and I'll let you know how that goes. Whichever batting you choose, just make sure you follow the manufacturer's instructions for washing and drying.

Backing

For my quilts, I cut and piece my quilt backings at least 6" larger than the quilt top (3" on all sides). Sometimes it doesn't work out quite that generously, but that is always my goal.

Labels

Quilts need labels. You've just made something fabulous, so why aren't you claiming some sort of credit or ownership over what you've created? Every quilt has a story and a label is part of the telling of it. Leaving the label off is like buying a book where half of the pages are empty—some important stuff is definitely missing. If nothing else, if you become famous, your kids will be able to sell it for a lot more money on eBay if they can prove you made it! If you won't think of yourself, think of your heirs! They'll thank you for labeling those quilts. The labels on my small quilts are machine stitched onto the backing fabric before quilting, while the labels on the big quilts are pieced, and then sewn into the backing itself.

As for what should be on the label, the answer is: whatever you want to include. My friend Karen Housner, a certified quilt appraiser, says that anything and everything I can do on the label to personalize it is a good thing. So my labels always include the following:

- The name of the quilt

- The name of the quiltmaker: that would be *moi*

- The name of the gloriously talented machine quilter who has had to work so hard to make me look better than I am

- Phoenix, Arizona, which is where I live

- The year and sometimes the month that the quilt was completed—especially if it's for a special occasion, event, or purpose

- Anything else I deem relevant at the time

- A favorite quotation

Label Quotations

As for the quotations that I include as part of the label, I'm not really sure why or when I started doing that. I just know that I've saved favorite quotes for as long as I can remember, and my quilts don't seem truly finished without a quotation. Some of my favorite quilts even got their names from the quotation included on the back. The really scary thing is that I think my selection of quotations might say something about my personality. Yikes!

You can judge for yourself since I've included the quote I used on each project along with the project instructions. Feel free to use your own selection of quotes for your quilts.

Quilting

Quilt as desired. That's what I tell my quilters.

I don't know much, but I know enough to get out of the way of someone who knows a lot more than I do about something. I've been blessed to have had several very talented and skilled machine quilters doing their best to make me look good. While the ladies who made most of the big quilts in this book don't need that kind of help, I usually do.

And for the record, just because I don't quilt, that doesn't mean I can't.

Binding

I like a relatively narrow binding, usually in a contrasting fabric. Left to my own devices, I usually use a bias-cut French (or double-fold) binding made with strips cut 2" wide and sewn on to the quilt with a ¼" seam allowance. With the light- to medium-weight battings I prefer, this strip-width and seam-allowance formula is usually perfect to completely fill the binding with batting while still allowing the folded edge of the binding to just cover the stitching.

BENNINGTON

Pieced by Nicole Reed. Quilted by Debbie Thornton.
Finished quilt size: 63½" x 63½" • Finished block size: 8½" x 8½"

Materials

18 assorted light 10" Layer Cake squares for blocks

47 assorted medium or dark 10" Layer Cake squares for blocks and outer border

½ yard of cream print for inner border

⅝ yard of fabric for binding

4 yards for backing

68" x 68" piece of batting

Cutting

From each of the 18 light squares, cut:
2 strips, 4¾" x 10"; crosscut into 4 squares, 4¾" x 4¾" (72 total)

From each of 36 medium or dark squares, cut:
1 strip, 4¾" x 10"; crosscut into 2 squares, 4¾" x 4¾" (72 total)
1 strip, 2½" x 10"; crosscut into 2 squares, 2½" x 2½" (72 total)
1 border strip, 2" x 10" (36 total)

From 1 medium or dark square, cut:
4 border squares, 5" x 5"

From each of the remaining 10 medium or dark squares, cut:
4 border strips, 2" x 10" (40 total)

From the inner-border fabric, cut:
6 strips, 2" x 42"

From the binding fabric, cut:
270" of 2"-wide bias binding

I'm a little predictable here in that I usually start by saying how I love this block and it's one of my favorites. I've always felt a little guilty about that, thinking it probably sounded a little bit insincere, as though, just maybe, one block might possibly be a little less of a favorite than another. And that's when it hit me. Nobody would ever ask parents with 12 children which one was their favorite! It would be assumed and accepted that each child was equally loved! Even if they were all loved a little differently, or for different reasons, they're all very well loved. So there!

Name: Bennington is a lovely little town in Kansas where Lynne Hagemeir, a fabric designer for Moda and the creative mind behind Kansas Troubles patterns, lives. I made the little quilt while I was "retreating" there a few years ago.

Making the Blocks

For each Bowtie block, you'll need the following pieces:

- **Background squares:** two matching light 4¾" squares

- **Bowtie squares:** two matching medium or dark 4¾" squares

- **Snowball corners:** two matching medium or dark 2½" squares

Use a scant ¼"-wide seam allowance throughout. After sewing each seam, press the seam allowances in the direction indicated by the arrows.

1. Referring to "Triangle Units" on page 12, draw a diagonal line from corner to corner on the wrong side of the 72 medium or dark 2½" squares.

2. Lay a marked square on the corner of a 4¾" light square, right sides together and raw edges aligned. Stitch along the drawn line and trim away the excess fabric, leaving a ¼" seam allowance.

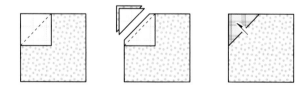

3. Lay out the pieces for each block in a four-patch arrangement as shown above right. Sew the pieces together in rows, and then sew the rows

together to complete a Bowtie block. Don't press the center seam just yet. Repeat to make a total of 36 blocks.

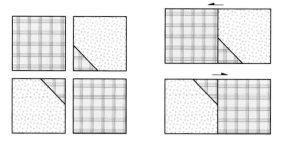

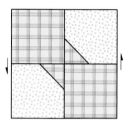

Make 36.

4. Use a seam ripper to remove two or three stitches from the seam allowance on both sides of the center seam, as shown.

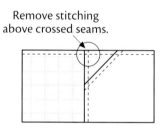

Remove stitching above crossed seams.

5. On the wrong side of the block, gently reposition the seam allowance to evenly distribute the fabric. Press the seam allowances in opposite directions, opening the seam allowances so that the center lies flat. When you look at the wrong side of the block, the seam allowances should be going in a counterclockwise direction around the center. The block should measure 9" square.

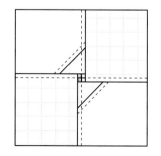

Assembling the Quilt Top

1. Lay out the blocks in six rows of six blocks each as shown in the quilt layout diagram.

2. Sew the blocks together into rows, pressing the seam allowances in opposite directions from one row to the next (or press them open). Then sew the rows together and press. The quilt top should measure 51½" x 51½".

Finishing the Quilt Top

1. Sew the 2"-wide inner-border strips together end to end. From the strip, cut four strips, 51½" long.

2. Sew two inner-border strips to the sides of the quilt top and press the seam allowances toward the borders.

3. Select one 2" x 10" border strip and cut it into four 2" squares.

4. Sew 2" squares from step 3 to both ends of the two remaining inner-border strips and press. Sew these borders to the top and bottom of the quilt top and press the seam allowances toward the borders.

5. Select 72 of the 2" x 10" border strips (you'll have three extra strips). Divide the strips into two sets of 36 strips each. Join the strips in one set together as shown and press the seam allowances in one direction (or press them open). The pieced strip should measure 10" x 54½". Repeat to make a second pieced strip.

Make 2.

6. Cut each pieced strip in half lengthwise to make a total of four pieced border strips, each measuring 5" x 54½".

7. Sew two border strips to the sides of the quilt top, keeping the pinked edges on the outside. Press the seam allowances toward the outer borders.

8. Sew 5" border squares to both ends of the two remaining border strips, keeping the pinked edges on the outside, and press. Sew these borders to the top and bottom of the quilt top and press the seam allowances toward the borders.

9. Refer to page 16 for finishing your quilt, or take it to your favorite long-arm quilter for finishing. Using the 2"-wide bias binding, make and attach binding.

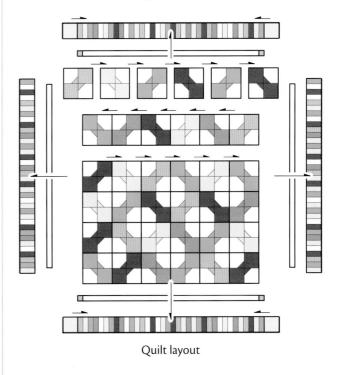

Quilt layout

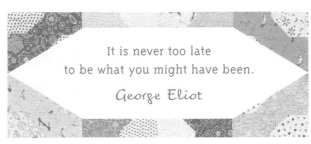

It is never too late
to be what you might have been.

George Eliot

Bennington
small quilt

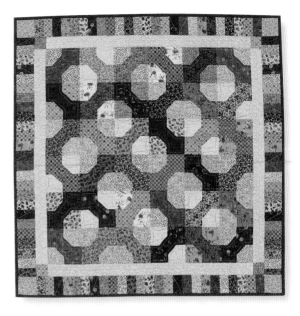

Pieced by Carrie Nelson. Quilted by Louise Haley.
Finished quilt size: 29½" x 29½"
Finished block size: 3¾" x 3¾"

Materials

18 assorted light 5" Charm Pack squares for blocks

55 assorted medium or dark 5" Charm Pack squares for blocks and outer border

¼ yard of cream print for inner border

⅓ yard of fabric for binding

1 yard of fabric for backing

34" x 34" piece of batting

Cutting

From *each* of the 18 light squares, cut:
2 strips, 2⅜" x 5"; crosscut into 4 squares,
   2⅜" x 2⅜" (72 total)

From *each* of 36 medium or dark squares, cut:
1 strip, 2⅜" x 5"; crosscut into 2 squares,
   2⅜" x 2⅜" (72 total)

1 strip, 1½" x 5"; crosscut into 2 squares,
   1½" x 1½" (72 total)

From 1 medium or dark square, cut:
2 strips, 1¾" x 5"; crosscut into 4 inner-border squares, 1¾" x 1¾"

From 1 medium or dark square, cut:
2 strips, 2½" x 5"; crosscut into 4 outer-border squares, 2½" x 2½"

From *each* of the 17 remaining medium or dark squares, cut:
3 border strips, 1½" x 5" (51 total)

From the inner-border fabric, cut:
4 strips, 1¾" x 23"

From the binding fabric, cut:
130" of 2"-wide bias binding

Making the Blocks

For each Bowtie block, you will need the following pieces:

- Background Squares: two matching light 2⅜" squares

- Bowtie Squares: two matching medium or dark 2⅜" squares

- Snowball Corners: two matching medium or dark 1½" squares

Use a scant ¼"-wide seam allowance throughout. For detailed instructions and illustrations on the following techniques refer to "Making the Blocks" on page 20.

1. Referring to "Triangle Units" on page 12, draw a diagonal line from corner to corner on the wrong side of the 72 medium or dark 1½" squares.

2. Lay a marked square on the corner of a light 2⅜" square, sew along the line, and trim.

3. Lay out the pieces for each block in a four-patch arrangement. Sew the pieces together in rows, and then sew the rows together to complete a Bowtie block. Repeat to make a total of 36 blocks measuring 4¼" square.

Assembling and Finishing the Quilt Top

For detailed instructions and illustrations on the following techniques refer to "Assembling the Quilt Top" and "Finishing the Quilt Top" on page 21.

1. Lay out the blocks in six rows of six blocks each. Sew the blocks together into rows, and then sew the rows together in the same manner as the larger quilt. The quilt top should measure 23" x 23".

2. Sew two of the 1¾"-wide inner-border strips to the sides of the quilt top and press the seam allowances toward the border. Sew 1¾" squares to both ends of the two remaining inner-border strips and press. Sew these borders to the top and bottom of the quilt top and press the seam allowances toward the border.

3. For the outer border, select 50 of the 1½" x 5" border strips (you'll have one extra strip). Divide the strips to make two sets of 25 strips. Join the strips in one set together and press the seam allowances in one direction (or press them open). The pieced strip should measure 5" x 25½". Repeat to make a second pieced strip.

4. Cut each pieced strip set in half lengthwise to yield a total of four pieced border strips, each measuring 2½" x 25½". Sew two pieced border strips to the sides of the quilt top, keeping the pinked edges on the outside. Press the seam allowances toward the outer border.

5. Sew 2½" outer-border squares to both ends of the two remaining outer-border strips, keeping the pinked edges on the outside, and press. Sew these borders to the top and bottom of the quilt top and press the seam allowances toward the border.

6. Refer to page 16 for finishing your quilt, or take it to your favorite long-arm quilter for finishing. Using the 2"-wide bias binding, make and attach binding.

Hot Cross

Pieced by Sue Maitre. Quilted by Diane Tricka.
Finished quilt size: 69½" x 69½" • Finished block size: 9½" x 9½"

Do you remember that puzzle thing I mentioned way back on page 6? This block is an example of my "MacGyver" process. Choosing a block I like is the easy part. The challenge comes from trying to figure out what size to cut the pieces and still fit everything into the square of fabric I have, while still being efficient. And figuring that all out is probably my favorite thing about these squares of fabric—but don't tell anyone because it involves a little bit of math. It always comes back to that, doesn't it?

Name: The blocks in this quilt reminded me of the wonderful rolls you find everywhere at Easter. And I like everything having to do with baked goods.

Materials

36 assorted 10" Layer Cake squares for blocks

46 assorted 10" Layer Cake squares for blocks and outer border

½ yard of cream print for inner border

⅝ yard of fabric for binding

4½ yards of fabric for backing

75" x 75" piece of batting

Cutting

From *each* of the 36 assorted squares for blocks:

1 square, 10" x 10"; cut into quarters diagonally to yield 4 triangles (144 total)

From *each* of 36 assorted squares for blocks and outer border, cut:

1 strip, 1½" x 10" (36 total), from the crosswise grain

6 strips, 1½" x 8", from the *lengthwise* grain; crosscut 1 *of the strips* into:

1 strip, 1½" x 5" (36 total)

1 square, 1½" x 1½" (36 total)

From 1 assorted square for blocks and outer border, cut:

1 strip, 2" x 10"; crosscut into 4 inner-border squares, 2" x 2"

5 border strips, 1½" x 10"

From 1 assorted square for blocks and outer border, cut:

4 outer-border squares, 5" x 5"

From *each* of the remaining 8 assorted squares for blocks and outer border, cut:

6 border strips, 1½" x 10" (48 total)

From the inner-border fabric, cut:

6 strips, 2" x 42"

From the binding fabric, cut:

290" of 2"-wide bias binding

Making the Blocks

For each block, you will need the following pieces:

- Four matching triangles
- Four matching 1½" x 8" strips
- One 1½" square

Use a scant ¼"-wide seam allowance throughout. After sewing each seam, press the seam allowances in the direction indicated by the arrows.

1. Lay out the pieces for each block as shown. Sew the pieces together in diagonal rows, and then sew the rows together to complete the block. Make a total of 36 blocks.

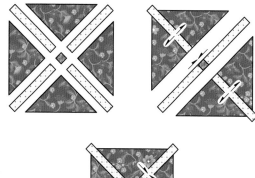

Make 36.

2. Position a 12½" square ruler with a 45° line on top of a block, centering the 45° line in the middle of the narrow strip. Align the 5" lines on the ruler horizontally and vertically with the points of the small center square and the 10" marks with the center of the narrow strips as shown above right.

Trim two sides of the block. Turn the block, realign the ruler, and trim the remaining sides. Each block should measure 10" square.

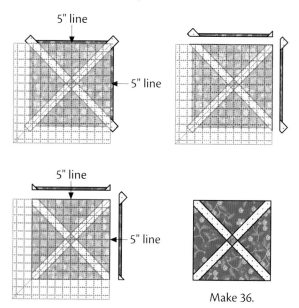

Make 36.

Assembling the Quilt Top

1. Lay out the blocks in six rows of six blocks each as shown in the quilt layout diagram. Sew the blocks together in rows and press the seam allowances in opposite directions from row to row (or press them open).

2. Sew the rows together and press the seam allowances in one direction (or press them open). The quilt top should measure 57½" x 57½".

Finishing the Quilt Top

1. Piece the 2"-wide inner-border strips together end to end. From the strips, cut four strips, 57½" long.

2. Sew two inner-border strips to the sides of the quilt top and press the seam allowances toward the borders.

3. Sew 2" squares to both ends of the two remaining inner-border strips and press. Sew these borders to the top and bottom of the quilt top and press the seam allowances toward the borders.

4. Sort the 1½"-wide border strips as follows:

- 89 strips, 1½" x 10" (you'll have 5 extra strips)

- 36 strips, 1½" x 8"

- 36 strips, 1½" x 5"

5. Cut the 1½" x 10" strips in half to make 168 strips measuring 1½" x 5". Trim the 8" strips to measure 1½" x 5". Re-sort the strips into four sets of 60 strips each, keeping as much variety as possible in each group.

6. Join the strips in one set together as shown and press the seam allowances in one direction (or press them open). The pieced strip should measure 5" x 60½". Repeat to make a total of four pieced outer-border strips.

Make 4.

7. Sew two outer-border strips to the sides of the quilt top, keeping the pinked edges on the outside. Press the seam allowances toward the outer borders.

8. Sew a 5" outer-border square to both ends of the two remaining outer-border strips, keeping the pinked edges on the outside and press. Sew these borders to the top and bottom of the quilt top and press the seam allowances toward the borders.

9. Refer to page 16 for finishing your quilt, or take it to your favorite long-arm quilter for finishing. Using the 2"-wide bias binding, make and attach binding.

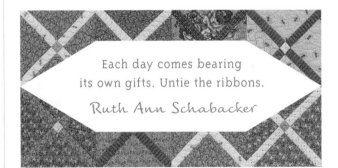

Each day comes bearing
its own gifts. Untie the ribbons.

Ruth Ann Schabacker

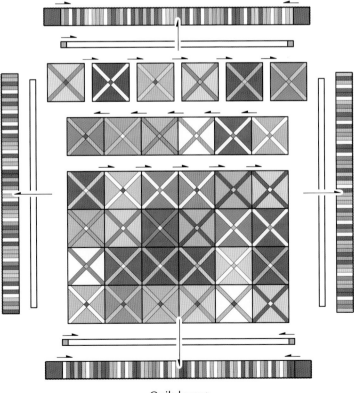

Quilt layout

HOT CROSS
small quilt

Pieced by Carrie Nelson. Quilted by Louise Haley.
Finished quilt size: 31½" x 31½"
Finished block size: 4½" x 4½"

Materials

50 assorted 5" Charm Pack squares for blocks

30 assorted 5" Charm Pack squares for outer border

¼ yard of cream print for inner border

⅓ yard of fabric for binding

1⅛ yards of fabric for backing

37" x 37" piece of batting

Cutting

Divide the 50 assorted Charm Pack squares for blocks into two groups of 25 squares. Use one group for the triangles in the blocks and the other group for the narrow strips.

From *each* of the 25 squares for the triangles, cut:
1 square, 5" x 5"; cut into quarters diagonally to yield 4 triangles (100 total)

From *each* of the 25 squares for narrow strips, cut:
4 strips, 1⅛" x 5", from the *lengthwise* grain; cut 1 of *the strips* into:

- 1 strip, 1⅛" x 3⅞" (25 total)
- 1 square, 1⅛" x 1⅛" (25 total)

From the inner-border fabric, cut:
4 strips, 1¾" x 23"

From 1 square for outer border, cut:
4 inner-border squares, 1¾" x 1¾"

From *each* of 25 squares for outer border, cut:
1 strip, 1½" x 5"; trim to 1½" x 3½" (25 total)
3 strips, 1½" x 3½" (75 total)

From *each* of the remaining 4 squares for outer border, cut:
1 square, 5" x 5"; cut into quarters diagonally to yield 4 triangles (16 total)

From the binding fabric, cut:
140" of 2"-wide bias binding

Making the Quilt Top

For each block, you'll need the following pieces:

- Four matching triangles

- Four matching strips, 1⅛" wide (there are two different lengths; three of the strips are oversized)

- One 1⅛" square

Use a scant ¼"-wide seam allowance throughout. For detailed instructions and illustrations on the following techniques refer to "Making the Blocks," "Assembling the Quilt Top," and "Finishing the Quilt Top" on pages 26 and 27.

1. Arrange and sew the pieces for each block together in diagonal rows, and then sew the rows together in the same manner as the larger block. Using a square ruler with a 45° line and aligning the 2½" lines on the ruler with the points of the center square, trim each block to measure 5" x 5". Make a total of 25 blocks.

2. Lay out the blocks in five rows of five blocks each. Sew the blocks together into rows, and then sew the rows together. The quilt top should measure 23" x 23".

3. Sew two 1¾"-wide inner-border strips to the sides of the quilt top and press the seam allowances toward the borders. Sew 1¾" squares to both ends of the two remaining inner-border strips and press. Sew these borders to the top and bottom of the quilt top and press the seam allowances toward the borders.

4. Sort the 1½" x 3½" strips into four sets of 25 strips each. Join the strips in one set together along their long edges and press the seam allowances in one direction (or press them open). The pieced strip should measure 3½" x 25½". Make a total of four pieced outer-border strips.

5. Sew two outer-border strips to the sides of the quilt top, pressing the seam allowances toward the outer border.

6. Using the 16 triangles for the border, arrange four different triangles as shown. Sew the triangles together in pairs along their short edges, and then sew the pairs together to make an hourglass unit. Trim the unit to 3½" square. Make four units.

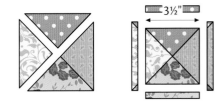

7. Sew an hourglass unit from step 6 to each end of each remaining outer-border strip. Press the seam allowances toward the border strip. Sew the strips to the top and bottom of the quilt top; press the seam allowances toward the outer border.

8. Refer to page 16 for finishing your quilt, or take it to your favorite long-arm quilter for finishing. Using the 2"-wide bias binding, make and attach binding.

IMAGINE

Pieced and quilted by Darlene Johannis.
Finished quilt size: 81¼" x 81¼" • Finished block size: 8½" x 8½"

I love the word "imagine." Those seven letters describe the power of your mind to create, to consider possibilities, to be adventurous, to be bold, and to invent. As quilters, we imagine every day. We see a fabric or pattern we love and we imagine a quilt. With apologies to John Lennon:

Imagine there's no difficult blocks, it's easy if you try. No bias edges below us, above us only squares. Imagine all the quilters, piecing for just one day. Imagine there's no ripping, it isn't hard to do. Nothing to stretch or pouf, and no funky corners too. Imagine all the quilters, living life in pieces!

Name: As I was finishing up the little quilt, one of the Davids on American Idol was singing "Imagine," and since the fabric collection is called Peace on Earth, it seemed like a sign.

Materials

48 assorted 10" Layer Cake squares for blocks

18 assorted 10" Layer Cake squares for outer border

2⅛ yards of white print for background and inner border

¾ yard of fabric for binding

5 yards of fabric for backing

86" x 86" piece of batting

Cutting

From the white print for background and inner border, cut:

10 strips, 4¾" x 42"; crosscut into 70 rectangles, 4¾" x 5¾" (6 will be extra)

8 border strips, 2⅝" x 42"

From each of 32 assorted squares for blocks, cut:

1 rectangle, 9" x 10" (32 total; don't worry about the pinked edges)

From each of the remaining 16 assorted squares for blocks, cut:

4 squares, 4¾" x 4¾" (64 total)

From each of the 18 assorted squares for outer border, cut:

2 rectangles, 4¾" x 10"; crosscut into 4 squares, 4¾" x 4¾" (72 total)

From the binding fabric, cut:
340" of 2"-wide bias binding

Making the Blocks

You'll be making two blocks at a time and will need the following pieces for each pair of blocks:

- One 9" x 10" assorted rectangle

- Two assorted matching or different 4¾" squares

- Two 4¾" x 5¾" background rectangles

Use a scant ¼"-wide seam allowance throughout. After sewing each seam, press the seam allowances in the direction indicated by the arrows.

1. Sew one 4¾" assorted square to one 4¾" x 5¾" background rectangle. Press the seam allowances toward the background rectangle. Repeat to make a second pieced strip.

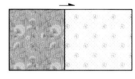

Make 2.

2. Sew the two pieced strips together as shown. (The placement of the squares isn't that important as long as the squares are in opposing corners, so if your piece is reversed, don't worry about it.)

3. Before pressing, in the center of the unit, clip the seam allowance to the seam line. Don't worry if you snip into the stitched line; eventually this will be trimmed off anyway. Press the seam allowances in opposite directions as shown.

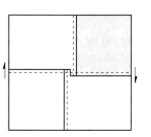

4. On the wrong side of the unit, use a pencil and ruler with a 45° line on it to draw a line from one corner on the rectangle and across the small square's seam intersection as shown. The key here is to draw a line across the rectangle and not across the small square. (Again, don't worry if your pieced rectangle is reversed; this will work as long as you draw a line across the rectangles and not across the squares.)

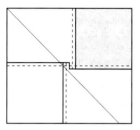

5. Draw a second line from the opposing corner, across the rectangles as shown. The lines will be approximately ½" apart.

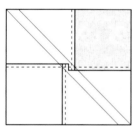

6. Place a 9" x 10" assorted rectangle right sides together with a pieced rectangle from step 5; align the edges and pin in place. The pinked edges will extend just a smidge on either end of the pieced rectangle; you can leave those for now. Sew on each of the drawn lines, and then cut between them as shown on the facing page. Trim the seam allowances to ¼" and press them toward the large triangle (or press them open).

Trim the block to measure 9" square, removing any pinked edges as necessary. Repeat to make a total of 64 blocks.

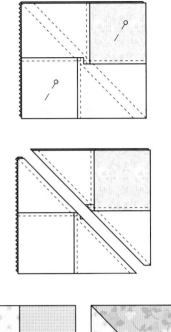

Make 64.

Assembling the Quilt Top

1. Lay out the blocks in eight rows of eight blocks each as shown in the quilt layout diagram.

2. Sew the blocks together into rows, pressing the seam allowances in opposite directions from one row to the next (or press them open). Then sew the rows together to complete the quilt top and press. The quilt top should measure 68½" x 68½".

Finishing the Quilt Top

1. Piece the 2⅝"-wide inner-border strips together end to end. From the strip, cut two strips, 68½" long. Sew these strips to the sides of the quilt top. Cut two more strips, 72¾" long, and sew them to the top and bottom of the quilt top. Press the seam allowances toward the just-added border.

2. Sort the 72 border squares into two sets of 17 squares each for the side borders and two sets of 19 squares each for the top and bottom borders. Sew each set of squares together to make a border strip. Press the seam allowances in one direction (or press them open). Make two 4¾" x 72¾" strips and sew them to the sides of the quilt top. Make two 4¾" x 81¼" strips and sew them to the top and bottom of the quilt top. Press the seam allowances toward the outer border.

3. Refer to page 16 for finishing your quilt, or take it to your favorite long-arm quilter for finishing. Using the 2"-wide bias binding, make and attach binding.

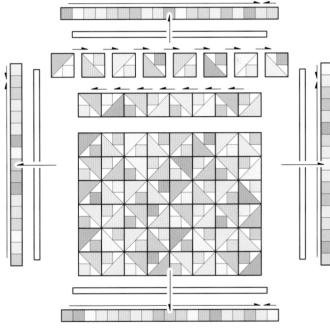

Quilt layout

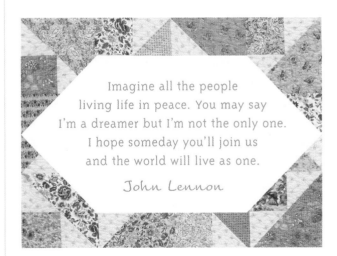

Imagine all the people
living life in peace. You may say
I'm a dreamer but I'm not the only one.
I hope someday you'll join us
and the world will live as one.

John Lennon

ÍMAGINE
small quilt

Pieced by Carrie Nelson. Quilted by Diane Tricka.
Finished quilt size: 37¼" x 37¼"
Finished block size: 3½" x 3½"

Materials

48 assorted 5" Charm Pack squares for blocks

38 assorted 5" Charm Pack squares for outer border

⅝ yard or cream print for background and inner border

⅓ yard of fabric for binding

1¼ yards of fabric for backing

42" x 42" piece of batting

Cutting

From the cream print for background and inner border, cut:

6 strips, 2¼" x 42"; crosscut into 72 rectangles, 2¼" x 3¼" (8 will be extra)

2 inner-border strips, 1⅜" x 30¼"

2 inner-border strips, 1⅜" x 28½"

From *each* of 32 assorted squares for blocks, cut:

1 rectangle, 4" x 5" (32 total; don't worry about the pinked edges)

From *each* of the remaining 16 assorted squares for blocks, cut:

2 strips, 2¼" x 5"; crosscut into 4 squares, 2¼" x 2¼" (64 total)

From *each* of the 38 assorted squares for outer border, cut:

2 border strips, 2¼" x 5" (76 total)

From the binding fabric, cut
150" of 2"-wide bias binding

Making the Blocks

You'll be making two blocks at a time and will need the following pieces for each pair of blocks:

- One 4" x 5" assorted rectangle

- Two assorted matching or different 2¼" squares

- Two 2¼" x 3¼" background rectangles

Use a scant ¼"-wide seam allowance throughout. For detailed instructions and illustrations on the following techniques refer to "Making the Blocks" on page 32.

1. Sew an assorted square to each background rectangle to make a pieced strip. Sew the pieced strips together in pairs in the same manner as the larger block.

2. Draw stitching lines across both pieced rectangles and stitch on both lines. Cut between the lines, trim the seam allowance to ¼", and press. The block should measure 4" square. Repeat to make a total of 64 blocks.

Assembling and Finishing the Quilt Top

For detailed instructions and illustrations on the following techniques refer to "Assembling the Quilt Top" and "Finishing the Quilt Top" on page 33.

1. Lay out the blocks in eight rows of eight blocks each. Sew the blocks together into rows, pressing the seam allowances in opposite directions from one row to the next (or press them open). Then sew the rows together to complete the quilt top and press. The quilt top should measure 28½" x 28½".

2. Sew the 28½"-long inner-border strips to the sides of the quilt top. Sew the 30¼"-long inner-border strips to the top and bottom of the quilt top. Press the seam allowances toward the just-added border.

3. For the outer border, join two 2¼" x 5" assorted border strips together along their long edges to make 38 strip sets. Press the seam allowances in one direction. From each strip set, cut two 2¼"-wide segments. Cut a total of 76 segments.

4. Sort the segments from step 3 into two sets of 17 segments each for the side borders and two sets of 21 segments each for the top and bottom borders. Sew each set of segments together as shown to make a border strip, pressing the seam allowances in one direction (or press them open). Sew the borders to the sides, and then to the top and bottom of the quilt top. Press the seam allowances toward the just-added borders.

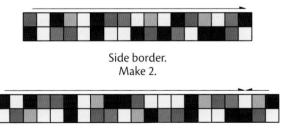

Side border.
Make 2.

Top/bottom border.
Make 2.

5. Refer to page 16 for finishing your quilt, or take it to your favorite long-arm quilter for finishing. Using the 2"-wide bias binding, make and attach binding.

LITTLE RED

Pieced by Judy Adams. Quilted by Diane Tricka.
Finished quilt size: 66¾" x 66¾" • Finished block size: 8⅞" x 8⅞"

A long time ago in an antique shop far away, I saw a quilt made with a block that looked very much like this one. Templates! No way—not going to do it—not me. But I really liked the block and there had to be a way to make it without templates. Hmmm... if I straighten that line there a bit, and straighten this one over here, this might work using some snowball corners. But how to get that pinwheel thing in opposing corners? Ugh. No. It can't be.... It's a math thing! Do you think there's some kind of secret conspiracy with math teachers? They keep finding ways to throw math curveballs at those of us who scoffed at ever actually needing math in our real lives.

Name: Several years ago, I made a quilt titled "Radio Flyer" using this block. When I made the little version of that quilt, I called it "Little Red." Maybe this one should be "Big Cream-Peach-Aqua-Green." Or maybe not.

Materials

36 assorted light 10" Layer Cake squares for blocks

36 assorted medium or dark 10" Layer Cake squares for blocks

2 yards of floral fabric for outer border and binding

½ yard of white print for inner border

4¼ yards of fabric for backing

72" x 72" piece of batting

Cutting

From *each* of 18 light squares, cut:
1 square, 9¾" x 9¾" (18 total)

From *each* of the remaining 18 light squares, cut:
1 strip, 4⅛" x 10"; crosscut into 2 squares, 4⅛" x 4⅛" (36 total)
1 strip, 3¾" x 10"; crosscut into 2 squares, 3¾" x 3¾" (36 total)

From *each* of 18 medium or dark squares, cut:
1 square, 9¾" x 9¾" (18 total)

From *each* of the remaining 18 medium or dark squares, cut:
1 strip, 4⅛" x 10"; crosscut into 2 squares, 4⅛" x 4⅛" (36 total)
1 strip, 3¾" x 10"; crosscut into 2 squares, 3¾" x 3¾" (36 total)

From the inner-border fabric, cut:
6 strips, 2" x 42"

From the outer-border and binding fabric, cut:
4 border strips, 5½" x 72", from the lengthwise grain*

280" of 2"-wide bias binding

*If you prefer crosswise grain strips, cut 8 border strips, 5½" x 42".

Making the Blocks

For each block, you'll need the following pieces:

- Two different 9¾" squares (one light and one medium or dark)

- Four different 4⅛" squares (two light and two medium or dark)

- Four different 3¾" squares (two light and two medium or dark)

Use a scant ¼"-wide seam allowance throughout. After sewing each seam, press the seam allowances in the direction indicated by the arrows.

1. Refer to "Triangle Units" on page 12 to draw a diagonal line from corner to corner on the wrong side of the 4⅛" and 3¾" squares. Place 4⅛" medium or dark squares on diagonally opposite corners of a 9¾" light square. Sew along the marked line and trim, leaving a ¼" seam allowance.

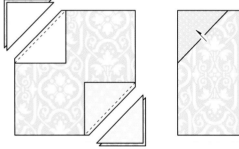

2. In the same manner, place marked 4⅛" light squares on diagonally opposite corners of a 9¾" medium or dark square. Sew and trim.

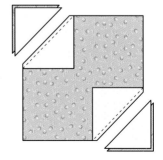

3. Repeat step 1, sewing the marked 3¾" medium or dark squares to the remaining corners of the light squares as shown. Make 18 light Snowball blocks. And yes, the snowballs are a little lopsided, but that's on purpose so that step 5 will work.

Make 18.

4. In the same manner, sew the marked 3¾" light squares to the remaining corners of the medium or dark squares. Make 18 dark Snowball blocks.

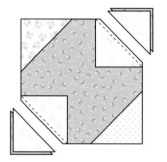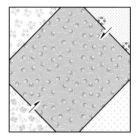

Make 18.

5. On the wrong side of the light Snowball blocks, draw a diagonal line from corner to corner across the larger triangles, as shown on the facing page. Layer a marked Snowball block right sides together with a dark Snowball block, *making sure that the snowball corners match the facing corners according to size*. The triangles should nestle into each other with the seam allowances abutting. Sew a scant ¼" on both sides of the marked line. Cut the squares apart on the line to make two blocks. Press the seam allowances toward the

darker side of the block (or press open). Repeat to make a total of 36 blocks. The blocks should measure 9⅜" square.

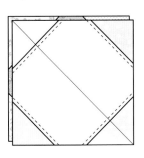

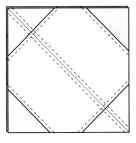

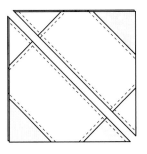

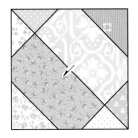

Make 36.

Assembling the Quilt Top

1. Lay out the blocks in six rows of six blocks each, rotating every other block 90° as shown in the quilt layout diagram.

2. Sew the blocks together in rows, pressing the seam allowances in opposite directions from one row to the next (or press them open). Then sew the rows together and press. The quilt top should measure 53¾" x 53¾".

Finishing the Quilt Top

1. Piece the 2"-wide inner-border strips together end to end. From the strips, cut two strips 53¾" long and sew them to opposite sides of the quilt top. Press the seam allowances toward the border. Cut two strips 56¾" long and sew them to the top and bottom of the quilt top; press.

2. Trim two of the 5½"-wide outer-border strips to measure 56¾" long. Sew the strips to opposite sides of the quilt top and press the seam allowances toward the outer border. Trim the remaining two strips to measure 66¾" long. Sew these borders to the top and bottom of the quilt top and press.

3. Refer to page 16 for finishing your quilt, or take it to your favorite long-arm quilter for finishing. Using the 2"-wide bias binding, make and attach binding.

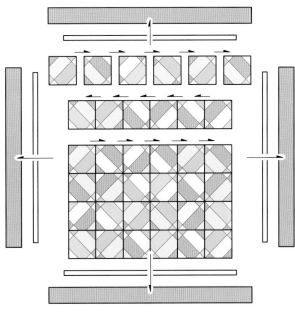

Quilt layout

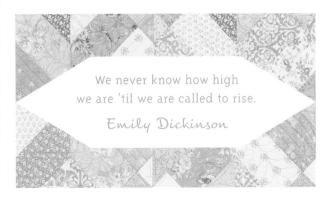

We never know how high
we are 'til we are called to rise.

Emily Dickinson

LITTLE RED
small quilt

Pieced by Carrie Nelson. Quilted by Louise Haley.
Finished quilt size: 29¼" x 37"
Finished block size: 3⅞" x 3⅞"

Materials

48 assorted light 5" Charm Pack squares for blocks

48 assorted medium or dark 5" Charm Pack squares for blocks

⅜ yard of medium or dark print for outer border

¼ yard of light print for inner border

⅓ yard of fabric for binding

1¼ yards of fabric for backing

34" x 42" piece of batting

Cutting

From *each* of 24 light squares, cut:
1 square, 4¾" x 4¾" (24 total)

From *each* of the remaining 24 light squares, cut:
1 strip, 2¼" x 5"; crosscut into 2 squares, 2¼" x 2¼" (48 total)
1 strip, 1⅞" x 5"; crosscut into 2 squares, 1⅞" x 1⅞" (48 total)

From *each* of 24 medium or dark squares, cut:
1 square, 4¾" x 4¾" (24 total)

From *each* of the remaining 24 medium or dark squares, cut:

1 strip, 2¼" x 5"; crosscut into 2 squares, 2¼" x 2¼" (48 total)

1 strip, 1⅞" x 5"; crosscut into 2 squares, 1⅞" x 1⅞" (48 total)

From the inner-border fabric, cut:

2 strips, 1¼" x 31½"

2 strips, 1¼" x 25¼"

From the outer-border fabric, cut:

2 strips, 2½" x 33"

2 strips, 2½" x 29¼"

From the binding fabric, cut:

150" of 2"-wide bias binding

Making the Blocks

For each pair of blocks, you'll need the following pieces:

- Two different 4¾" squares (one light and one medium or dark)

- Four different 2¼" squares (two light and two medium or dark)

- Four different 1⅞" squares (two light and two medium or dark)

Use a scant ¼"-wide seam allowance throughout. For detailed instructions and illustrations on the following techniques refer to "Making the Blocks" on page 38.

1. Refer to "Triangle Units" on page 12 to draw a diagonal line from corner to corner on the wrong side of the 2¼" and 1⅞" squares. Sew marked 2¼" medium or dark squares on diagonally opposite corners of a 4¾" light square. In the same manner, sew marked 2¼" light squares on diagonally opposite corners of a 4¾" medium or dark square.

2. Repeat step 1, sewing the marked 1⅞" medium or dark squares to the remaining corners of the light squares. Make 24 light Snowball blocks. In the same manner, sew the marked 1⅞" light squares

to the remaining corners of the medium or dark squares. Make 24 dark Snowball blocks.

3. On the wrong side of the light Snowball blocks, draw a diagonal line from corner to corner across the larger triangles. Layer a marked Snowball block right sides together with a dark Snowball block, *making sure that the snowball corners match the facing corners according to size*. The triangles should nestle into each other with the seam allowances abutting. Sew a scant ¼" on both sides of the marked line. Cut the square apart on the line to make two blocks. Press the seam allowances toward the darker side of the block (or press open). Repeat to make a total of 48 blocks. The blocks should measure 4⅜" square.

Assembling and Finishing the Quilt Top

For detailed instructions and illustrations on the following techniques refer to "Assembling the Quilt Top" and "Finishing the Quilt Top" on page 39.

1. Lay out the blocks in eight rows of six blocks each; rotate every other block 90° as shown in the photo on page 40. Sew the blocks together into rows, pressing the seam allowances in opposite directions from one row to the next (or press them open). Then sew the rows together and press. The quilt top should measure 23¾" x 31½".

2. Sew the 31½"-long inner-border strips to opposite sides of the quilt top and press the seam allowances toward the border. Sew the 25¼"-long inner-border strips to the top and bottom of the quilt top and press.

3. Sew the 33"-long outer-border strips to opposite sides of the quilt top and press the seam allowances toward the border. Sew the 29¼"-long border strips to the top and bottom of the quilt top and press.

4. Refer to page 16 for finishing your quilt, or take it to your favorite long-arm quilter for finishing. Using the 2"-wide bias binding, make and attach binding.

Pieced by Lisa Durst. Quilted by Cindy Paulsgrove.
Finished quilt size: 61½" x 61½" • Finished block size: 8" x 8"

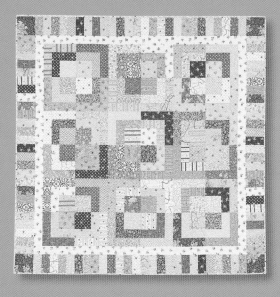

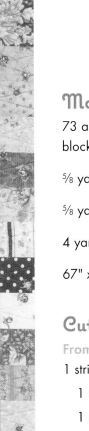

If you've made a few quilts, you've probably made a Log Cabin block or two somewhere, or at least some variation of it. I love Log Cabin blocks because they're pretty foolproof, and I'm all about making things as easy as possible. If nothing else, I'm way too old to be making things harder than they need to be. Not that I don't try anyway, just not with this quilt.

Name: The fabric collection for the little quilt is called American Primer, and the word "primer" means a lesson book or reader. And the most famous reader I know is the *McGuffey Reader.* Which, by the way, I am way too young to have actually used in school.

Materials

73 assorted 10" Layer Cake squares for blocks and outer border

⅝ yard of white print for inner border

⅝ yard of fabric for binding

4 yards of fabric for backing

67" x 67" piece of batting

Cutting

From *each* of 36 assorted squares, cut:

1 strip, 4½" x 10"; crosscut into:

    1 square, 4½" x 4½" (36 total)

    1 strip, 2½" x 4½" (36 total)

2 strips, 2½" x 10"; crosscut *1 of the strips* to 6½" long (36 total; set the remaining 36 strips aside for the outer border)

From *each* of 36 assorted squares, cut:

3 strips, 2½" x 10"; crosscut into:

    1 strip, 2½" x 6½" (36 total)

    1 strip, 2½" x 8½" (36 total)

(Set the remaining 36 strips aside for the outer border.)

From the 1 remaining assorted square, cut:

4 border squares, 5" x 5"

From the inner-border fabric, cut:

6 strips, 2½" x 42"

From the binding fabric, cut:

260" of 2"-wide bias binding

Making the Blocks

For each block, you'll need the following pieces:

- One assorted 4½" square

- One assorted 2½" x 4½" strip and one matching 2½" x 6½" strip

- One assorted 2½" x 6½" strip and one matching 2½" x 8½" strip

Use a scant ¼"-wide seam allowance throughout. After sewing each seam, press the seam allowances in the direction indicated by the arrows.

1. Join a 2½" x 4½" strip to one side of a 4½" square. Join a matching 2½" x 6½" strip to the top of the square as shown. The unit should measure 6½" square.

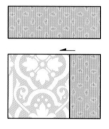 

2. Join a 2½" x 6½" strip to one side of the unit from step 1. Join a matching 2½" x 8½" strip to top of the unit to complete a Log Cabin block. Make a total of 36 blocks. The blocks should measure 8½" square.

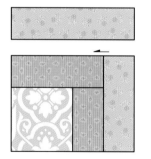 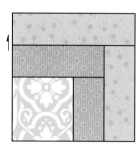

Make 36.

Assembling the Quilt Top

1. Lay out the blocks in six rows of six blocks each; rotate every other block 90° as shown in the quilt layout diagram.

2. Sew the blocks together into rows, pressing the seam allowances in opposite directions from one row to the next (or press them open). Then sew the rows together and press. The quilt top should measure 48½" x 48½".

Finishing the Quilt Top

1. Piece the 2½"-wide inner-border strips together end to end. From the strip, cut two 48½"-long strips for the side borders, and two 52½"-long strips for the top and bottom borders. Sew the borders to the sides, and then the top and bottom of the quilt top. Press the seam allowances toward the just-added border.

2. Sort the 2½" x 10" border strips into two sets of 26 strips each. Yes, there will be 20 strips left over so pick the strips you like best. Join the strips in one set together as shown and press the seam allowances in one direction (or press them open). The pieced strip should measure 10" x 52½". Repeat to make a second pieced strip.

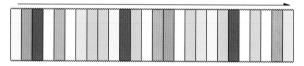

Make 2.

3. Cut each pieced strip set in half lengthwise to make a total of four pieced outer-border strips, each measuring 5" x 52½".

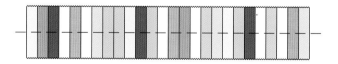

4. Sew two outer-border strips to the sides of the quilt top, keeping the pinked edges on the outside. Press the seam allowances toward the outer border.

5. Sew 5" border squares to both ends of the two remaining border strips, keeping the pinked edges on the outside, and press. Sew these borders to the top and bottom of the quilt top and press the seam allowances toward the outer border.

6. Refer to page 16 for finishing your quilt, or take it to your favorite long-arm quilter for finishing. Using the 2"-wide bias binding, make and attach binding.

Do what you can, with what you have, where you are.

Theodore Roosevelt

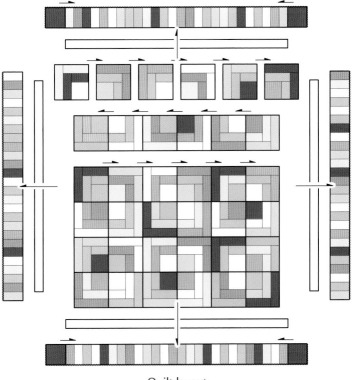

Quilt layout

McGuffey
small quilt

Pieced by Carrie Nelson. Quilted by Louise Haley.
Finished quilt size: 31½" x 31½"
Finished block size: 4" x 4"

Materials

72 assorted 5" Charm Pack squares for blocks and outer border

8 assorted 5" Charm Pack squares for outer border

⅓ yard of white print for inner border

⅓ yard of fabric for binding

1⅛ yards of fabric for backing

37" x 37" piece of batting

Cutting

From *each* of 36 assorted squares, cut:
1 strip, 2½" x 5"; crosscut into:
    1 square, 2½" x 2½" (36 total)
    1 strip, 1½" x 2½" (36 total)
1 strip, 1½" x 3½" (36 total)

From *each* of the remaining 36 assorted squares, cut:
3 strips, 1½" x 5"; crosscut into:
    1 strip, 1½" x 4½" (36 total)
    1 strip, 1½" x 3½" (36 total)
(Set the remaining 36 strips aside for the outer border.)

From 1 of the squares for outer border, cut:
4 border squares, 2½" x 2½"

From *each* of the remaining 7 squares for outer border, cut:
3 border strips, 1½" x 5" (21 total)

From the inner-border fabric, cut:
2 strips, 2" x 27½"
2 strips, 2" x 24½"

From the binding fabric, cut:
140" of 2"-wide bias binding

Making the Quilt Top

For each block, you'll need the following pieces:

- One assorted 2½" square

- One assorted 1½" x 2½" strip and one matching 1½" x 3½" strip

- One assorted 1½" x 3½" strip and one matching 1½" x 4½" strip

Use a scant ¼"-wide seam allowance throughout. For detailed instructions and illustrations on the following techniques, refer to "Making the Blocks," "Assembling the Quilt Top," and "Finishing the Quilt Top" on pages 44 and 45.

1. Join a 1½" x 2½" strip to one side of a 2½" square. Join a matching 1½" x 3½" strip to the top of the square in the same manner as the larger block. The unit should measure 3½" square.

2. Join a 1½" x 3½" strip to one side of the unit from step 1. Join a matching 1½" x 4½" strip to top of the unit to complete a Log Cabin block. Make a total of 36 blocks. The blocks should measure 4½" square.

3. Lay out the blocks in six rows of six blocks each; rotate every other block 90° as shown in the photo on page 46. Sew the blocks together into rows, pressing the seam allowances in opposite directions from one row to the next (or press them open). Then sew the rows together and press. The quilt top should measure 24½" x 24½".

4. Sew the 24½"-long inner-border strips to opposite sides of the quilt top and press the seam allowances toward the border. Sew the 27½"-long inner-border strips to the top and bottom of the quilt top and press.

5. Sort 54 of the 1½" x 5" border strips into two sets of 27 strips each (you'll have 3 extra strips). Join the strips in one set together along their long edges and press the seam allowances in one direction (or press them open). The pieced strip should measure 5" x 27½". Repeat to make a second pieced strip.

6. Cut each pieced strip set in half lengthwise to make a total of four outer-border strips, each measuring 2½" x 27½".

7. Sew two outer-border strips to the sides of the quilt top, keeping the pinked edges on the outside. Press the seam allowances toward the outer border.

8. Sew 2½" border squares to both ends of the two remaining border strips, keeping the pinked edges on the outside and press. Sew these borders to the top and bottom of the quilt top and press the seam allowances toward the outer border.

9. Refer to page 16 for finishing your quilt, or take it to your favorite long-arm quilter for finishing. Using the 2"-wide bias binding, make and attach binding.

Pieced by Lissa Alexander. Quilted by Maggi Honeyman.
Finished quilt size: 78" x 78" • Finished block size: 12" x 12"

Delightful. Delicious. De-lovely. Okay, I know that's not really a word but I like the alliteration and the song. Work with me here…it's delectable. All of those lovely words apply to blocks with lots of half-square triangles, like this Mountain thing here. And before you start moaning and groaning about all the half-square triangles in this quilt, consider two things. These are big. That makes them easy. And there aren't that many of them. You're going to be making eight at a time. And this is the only quilt that has half-square triangles. Okay, so that was five things; I got on a roll. Besides, you wouldn't be reading this if you didn't like them too.

Name: Bon Jovi. Nice Day. iPod. Cute guy, cute quilt. I take signs seriously. "When the world gets in my way…I say…have a nice day."

Materials

6 fat quarters of assorted light prints for background

36 assorted medium or dark 10" Layer Cake squares for blocks

14 assorted medium 10" Layer Cake squares for setting triangles

2 dark 10" Layer Cake squares for setting triangles

21 assorted 10" Layer Cake squares for border

⅝ yard of fabric for binding

5 yards of fabric for backing

83" x 83" piece of batting

Cutting

From *each* of the light prints for background, cut:

2 squares, 10" x 10" (12 total)

4 squares, 4½" x 4½" (24 total)

From *each* of the 14 medium squares and 2 dark squares for setting triangles, cut:

1 square, 10" x 10"; cut in half diagonally to yield 2 triangles (32 total)

From 1 medium or dark square for border, cut:

4 border squares, 5" x 5" (don't worry about the pinked edges)

From *each* of the 20 remaining squares for border, cut:

4 border strips, 2¼" x 10" (80 total)

From the binding fabric, cut:

325" of 2"-wide bias binding

Making the Blocks

For each pair of blocks, you'll need the following pieces:

• Background: one 10" square and two 4½" squares, all matching

- **Small half-square triangles:** one medium **or** dark 10" square

- **Large half-square triangles:** one medium and one dark 10" square **or** four different triangles (see step 3)

Use a scant ¼"-wide seam allowance throughout. After sewing each seam, press the seam allowances in the direction indicated by the arrows.

1. Draw intersecting diagonal lines from corner to corner on the wrong side of a 10" background square. Layer the marked square with a 10" medium or dark square, right sides together and raw edges aligned. Stitch a scant ¼" on each side of both drawn diagonal lines.

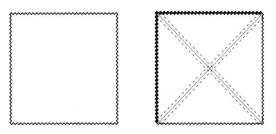

2. Carefully cut the square apart horizontally and vertically as shown to yield four 5" squares. Then cut the squares apart on the drawn diagonal lines to yield eight half-square-triangle units. Trim the units to measure 4½" square. Repeat to make a total of 96 half-square-triangle units.

Cut.

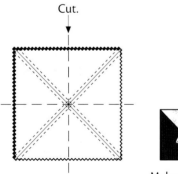

Make 96 total.

3. To piece the large half-square-triangle units, you can cut the 10" squares in half diagonally, and then randomly sew a medium triangle and a dark triangle together along their long edges. Or, you can draw a diagonal line from corner to corner on the wrong side of a 10" medium square. Layer the marked square with a 10" dark square, right sides

together and raw edges aligned. Stitch a scant ¼" on each side of the drawn line as shown. Then cut the squares apart on the drawn line. Make a total of 24 half-square-triangle units and trim them to measure 8½" square.

Cut.

Make 24.

4. Using four matching half-square-triangle units from step 2, sew together two units and one 4½" light square as shown. Then sew the two remaining units together as shown.

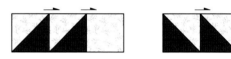

5. Lay out the units from step 4 and one half-square-triangle unit from step 3 as shown. Sew the units together in rows, and then sew the rows together to complete the block. Repeat to make a total of 24 blocks. The block should measure 12½" square.

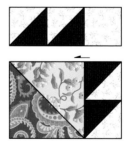

Make 24.

6. Join two medium setting triangles along their short edges to make eight large triangles; don't worry about the pinked edges.

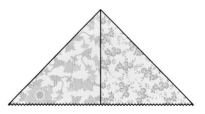

Make 8.

7. Join a medium triangle and a dark triangle along their long edges. Then sew medium triangles to adjacent sides of the unit as shown to make a corner triangle. Make four corner triangles.

Make 4.

Assembling the Quilt Top

1. Lay out the blocks and setting triangles in diagonal rows, rotating the blocks as shown in the quilt layout diagram.

2. Sew the blocks and setting triangles together into rows, pressing the seam allowances in the opposite direction from row to row (or press them open). The setting triangles are oversized and will be trimmed after the quilt top is assembled.

3. Sew the rows together and press the seam allowances in one direction (or press them open). Add the corner triangles last, press the seam allowances toward the triangles.

Finishing the Quilt Top

1. Before you can attach the border, you're going to have to trim the edges of the quilt top so that they are straight and even and the corners are square. I never have to do this, but everybody else usually does. (Just checking; I want to see if you're really reading this or just looking at the diagrams.) To trim and straighten the quilt top, align the $\frac{3}{8}$" line on your long ruler with the outermost points of the blocks. Use a rotary cutter to trim any excess fabric, leaving a $\frac{3}{8}$"-wide seam allowance and making sure the corners are square. The trimmed quilt should measure $68\frac{3}{4}$" x $68\frac{3}{4}$" for the pieced border to fit properly.

2. Select 78 of the $2\frac{1}{4}$" x 10" border strips (you'll have two extra strips). Divide the strips into two sets of 39 strips each. Join the strips in one set together as shown and press the seam allowances in one direction (or press them open). The pieced strip should measure 10" x $68\frac{3}{4}$". Repeat to make a second pieced strip. Cut each pieced strip set in half lengthwise to make a total of four outer-border strips, each measuring 5" x $68\frac{3}{4}$".

Make 2.

3. Sew two outer-border strips to the sides of the quilt top, keeping the pinked edges on the outside. Press the seam allowances toward the border.

4. Sew 5" border squares to both ends of the two remaining outer-border strips, keeping the pinked edges on the outside, and press. Sew these borders to the top and bottom of the quilt top and press the seam allowances toward the border.

5. Refer to page 16 for finishing your quilt, or take it to your favorite long-arm quilter for finishing. Using the 2"-wide bias binding, make and attach binding.

Quilt layout

NICE DAY
small quilt

Pieced by Carrie Nelson. Quilted by Louise Haley.
Finished quilt size: 32½" x 32½"
Finished block size: 4½" x 4½"

Materials

2 fat quarters of assorted light prints for backgrounds

36 assorted medium or dark 5" Charm Pack squares for blocks

16 assorted medium 5" Charm Pack squares for setting triangles

30 assorted 5" Charm Pack squares for border

⅓ yard of fabric for binding

1¼ yards of fabric for backing

38" x 38" piece of batting

Cutting

From each of the light prints for background, cut:
6 squares, 5" x 5" (12 total)
12 squares, 2" x 2" (24 total)

From each of the 16 medium squares for setting triangles, cut:
1 square, 5" x 5"; cut in half diagonally to yield 2 triangles (32 total)

From each of 26 assorted squares for border, cut:
1 border strip, 1½" x 5"; trim to 3½" long (26 total)
3 border strips, 1½" x 3½" (78 total)

From each of the 4 remaining assorted squares for border, cut:
1 border square, 3½" x 3½" (4 total)

From the binding fabric, cut:
145" of 2"-wide bias binding

Making the Blocks

For each pair of blocks, you'll need the following pieces:

- **Background:** one 5" square and two 2" squares, all matching

- **Small half-square triangles:** one medium or dark 5" square

- **Large half-square triangles:** one medium and one dark 5" square **or** four different triangles (see step 3)

Use a scant ¼"-wide seam allowance throughout. For detailed instructions and illustrations on the following techniques, refer to "Making the Blocks" on page 49.

1. Draw intersecting diagonal lines from corner to corner on the wrong side of a 5" background square. Layer the marked square with a 5" medium or dark square, right sides together and raw edges aligned. Stitch a scant ¼" on each side of *both* drawn diagonal lines.

2. Carefully cut the square apart horizontally and vertically to yield four 2½" squares in the same manner as the larger block. Then cut the squares apart on the drawn diagonal lines to yield eight half-square-triangle units. Trim units to measure 2" square. Repeat to make a total of 96 half-square-triangle units.

3. To piece the large half-square-triangle units, you can cut the 5" squares in half diagonally and then randomly sew a medium triangle and a dark triangle together along their long edges. Or, you can draw a diagonal line from corner to corner on the wrong side of a 5" medium square. Layer the marked square with a dark square, right sides together and raw edges aligned. Stitch a scant ¼" on each side of the drawn line, and then cut the squares apart on the drawn line. Make a total of 24 half-square-triangle units and trim them to measure 3½" square.

4. Lay out four 2" half-square-triangle units, one 3½" half-square-triangle unit, and one 2" square as shown in the diagrams on page 50 (steps 4 and 5), and then sew the pieces together as described. Repeat to make a total of 24 blocks. The block should measure 5" square.

5. Join 16 medium setting triangles together in pairs along their short edges to make 8 large triangles; don't worry about the pinked edges.

6. Join two medium triangles together along their long edges. Then sew medium triangles to adjacent sides of the unit as shown on page 51 to make a corner triangle. Make four corner triangles.

Assembling and Finishing the Quilt Top

For detailed instructions and illustrations on the following techniques, refer to "Assembling the Quilt Top" and "Finishing the Quilt Top" on page 51.

1. Lay out the blocks and setting triangles in diagonal rows, rotating the blocks as shown in the photo. Sew the blocks and setting triangles together into rows, pressing the seam allowances in the opposite direction from row to row (or press them open). The setting triangles are oversized and will be trimmed after the quilt top is assembled.

2. Sew the rows together and press the seam allowances in one direction (or press them open). Add the corner triangles last; press the seam allowances toward the triangles.

3. To trim and straighten the quilt top, align the ½" line on your long ruler with the outermost points of the blocks. Use a rotary cutter to trim any excess fabric, leaving a ½"-wide seam allowance and making sure the corners are square. The trimmed quilt should measure 26½" x 26½" for the pieced border to fit properly.

4. Divide the 1½" x 3½" border strips into four sets of 26 strips each. Join the strips in one set together along their long edges and press the seam allowances in one direction (or press them open). The pieced strip should measure 3½" x 26½". Make a total of four outer-border strips.

5. Sew two outer-border strips to the sides of the quilt top, pressing the seam allowances toward the border.

6. Sew 3½" border squares to both ends of the two remaining border strips and press. Sew these borders to the top and bottom of the quilt top and press the seam allowances toward the border.

7. Refer to page 16 for finishing your quilt, or take it to your favorite long-arm quilter for finishing. Using the 2"-wide bias binding, make and attach binding.

Pieced by Judy Adams. Quilted by Diane Tricka.
Finished quilt size: 68½" x 81½" • Finished block size: 4" x 8"

Some of my favorite quilts were inspired by antique two-color quilts. In this case, the colors were rusty orange and brownish gold. I'm serious! I'm thinking that might have something to do with why it was in such good condition. Since I'm not a "strict reproductionist," it was easy to start making some changes. Two fabrics? Gone. Original color choice? Gone. Straight, plain strips? Gone. Proportion of the strips and geese? Gone. As you can see, I'm not very strict about a lot of things.

Name: Flying geese are always in season at my house.

Materials

1⅞ yards of light print for Flying Geese blocks and sashing

58 assorted 10" Layer Cake squares for Flying Geese blocks, sashing, and border

⅝ yard of fabric for binding

5¼ yards of fabric for backing

74" x 87" piece of batting

Cutting

From the light print, cut:
9 strips, 4⅞" x 42"; crosscut into 72 squares, 4⅞" x 4⅞"
6 strips, 2½" x 42"

From *each* of 18 medium or dark squares, cut:
1 square, 9¼" x 9¼" (18 total)

From *each* of 32 assorted squares, cut:
1 border strip, 5" x 10" (32 total), from the lengthwise grain
1 sashing strip, 4" x 10" (32 total)

From *each* of the 8 remaining assorted squares, cut:
2 sashing strips, 4" x 10" (16 total), from the lengthwise grain

From the binding fabric, cut:
310" of 2"-wide bias binding

Assembling the Quilt Top

Use a scant ¼"-wide seam allowance throughout. After sewing each seam, press the seam allowances in the direction indicated by the arrows or you can press the seam allowances open.

1. Refer to "Flying-Geese Units" on page 13. Use four matching 4⅞" light squares and one 9¼" medium or dark square to make one set of four matching Flying Geese blocks. The blocks should measure 4½" x 8½". Make a total of 18 sets of four matching Flying Geese blocks (72 total).

Make 72.

2. Sort the blocks into four groups of 18 blocks each; there should be one Flying Geese block from each fabric in each group. Randomly sew the blocks in one group together as shown to make a strip measuring 8½" x 72½". Repeat to make a total of four Flying Geese strips. (The arrangement of the blocks in each strip should be different.)

Make 4.

3. Divide the 4" x 10" sashing strips into six sets of eight strips each. Using one set of strips, join the strips end to end to make a strip measuring about 76" long. Repeat to make a second 76" long strip. Lay out the two strips side by side, offsetting the position of the seam line in the two strips, and trim both strips to measure 72½" long. Repeat to make a total of three trimmed pairs of pieced strips.

4. Sew the 2½"-wide light strips together end to end. From the strip, cut three 72½"-long strips.

5. Using a pair of pieced strips from step 3, sew the strips to both long sides of a light strip from step 4 as shown. The strip should measure 9½" x 72½". Repeat to make a total of three sashing strips.

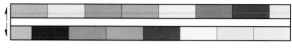

Make 3.

6. Lay out the Flying Geese strips and the sashing strips, alternating them as shown in the layout diagram. Sew the strips together, pressing the seam allowances toward the sashing strips. The quilt top should measure 59½" x 72½".

Finishing the Quilt Top

1. Sort the 5" x 10" border strips into four sets of eight strips each. Join the strips in one set together end to end as shown, keeping the pinked edges on the outside, to make a border strip. Press the seam allowances in one direction (or press them open). Repeat to make a total of four border strips, each measuring about 76" long.

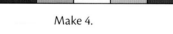

Make 4.

2. Trim two border strips to measure 72½" long and sew them to the sides of the quilt top. Press the seam allowances toward the border. Trim the remaining two border strips to measure 68½" long and sew them to the top and bottom of the quilt top. Press the seam allowances toward the border.

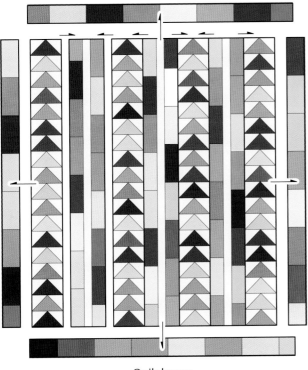

Quilt layout

3. Refer to page 16 for finishing your quilt, or take it to your favorite long-arm quilter for finishing. Using the 2"-wide bias binding, make and attach binding.

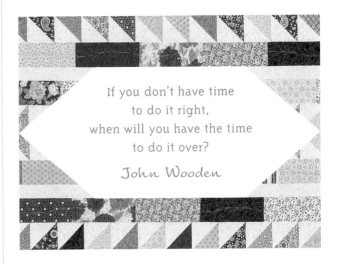

If you don't have time
to do it right,
when will you have the time
to do it over?

John Wooden

OPEN SEASON
small quilt

Pieced by Carrie Nelson. Quilted by Louise Haley.
Finished quilt size: 28½" x 34½"
Finished block size: 1½" x 3"

Materials

⅝ yard of cream print for Flying Geese blocks and sashing

58 assorted 5" Charm Pack squares for Flying Geese blocks, sashing, and border

⅓ yard of fabric for binding

1⅛ yards of fabric for backing

34" x 40" piece of batting

Cutting

From the cream print, cut:

5 strips, 2⅜" x 42"; crosscut into 80 squares, 2⅜" x 2⅜"

3 strips, 1½" x 30½"

From *each* of 20 medium or dark squares, cut:

1 square, 4¼" x 4¼" (20 total)

From *each* of 28 assorted squares, cut:

1 border strip, 2½" x 5" (28 total), from the *lengthwise* grain (don't worry about the pinked edges)

1 sashing strip, 2" x 5" (28 total)

58

From *each* of the 10 remaining assorted squares, cut:

2 sashing strips, 2" x 5" (20 total), from the *lengthwise* grain

From the binding fabric, cut:

140" of 2"-wide bias binding

Assembling and Finishing the Quilt Top

Use a scant ¼"-wide seam allowance throughout. For detailed instructions and illustrations on the following techniques refer to "Assembling the Quilt Top" and "Finishing the Quilt Top" on page 56.

1. Refer to "Flying-Geese Units" on page 13. Use four 2⅜" cream squares and one 4¼" medium or dark square to make one set of four matching Flying Geese blocks. The blocks should measure 2" x 3½". Make a total of 20 sets of four matching flying geese (80 total).

2. Sort the blocks into four groups of 20 blocks each; there should be one Flying Geese block from each fabric in each group. Randomly sew the blocks in one group together to make a strip measuring 3½" x 30½". Repeat to make a total of four Flying Geese strips. (The arrangement of the blocks in each strip should be different.)

3. Divide the 2" x 5" sashing strips into six sets of eight strips each. Using one set of strips, join the strips end to end to make a strip measuring about 36" long. Repeat to make a second 36"-long strip. Lay out the two strips side by side, offsetting the position of the seam line in the two strips, and trim both strips to measure 30½" long. Repeat to make a total of three trimmed pairs of pieced strips.

4. Sew a pair of sashing strips from step 3 to both long sides of a 1½"-wide cream strip. The strip should measure 4½" x 30½". Repeat to make a total of three sashing strips.

5. Lay out the Flying Geese strips and the sashing strips, alternating them as shown in the photo on page 58. Sew the strips together, pressing the seam allowances toward the sashing strips. The quilt top should measure 24½" x 30½".

6. Sort the 2½" x 5" border strips into four sets of seven strips each. Join the strips in one set together end to end, keeping the pinked edges on the outside, to make a border strip. Press the seam allowances in one direction (or press them open). Repeat to make a total of four border strips, each measuring about 31" long.

7. Trim two border strips from step 6 to measure 30½" long and sew them to the sides of the quilt top. Press the seam allowances toward the border. Trim the remaining two border strips to measure 28½" long and sew them to the top and bottom of the quilt top. Press the seam allowances toward the border.

8. Refer to page 16 for finishing your quilt, or take it to your favorite long-arm quilter for finishing. Using the 2"-wide bias binding, make and attach binding.

PLAN C

Pieced by Judy Adams. Quilted by Diane Tricka.
Finished quilt size: 77½" x 77½" • Finished flying-geese-unit size: 4" x 8" • Finished four-patch-unit size: 8" x 8"

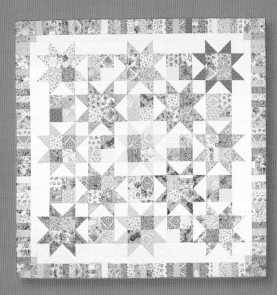

Starry, starry quilt. Paint your palette pink and green. I love star quilts in all their variations, sizes, and configurations. I think that makes me a bit star-struck. So twinkle, twinkle, pretty star, you must be my lucky star... I just think of you and I start to sew.

Name: Every quilt starts with a plan. Not every quilt goes according to plan. Some quilts have more than one plan. This quilt had more than three plans but this was the letter that sounded best for the name of my quilt.

Materials

2⅝ yards of white print for block background and inner border

59 assorted 10" Layer Cake squares for blocks and outer border

⅝ yard of fabric for binding

7¼ yards of fabric for backing

83" x 83" piece of batting

Cutting

From the white print, cut:

4 strips, 9¼" x 42"; crosscut into 13 squares, 9¼" x 9¼"

1 strip, 8½" x 42"; crosscut into 8 rectangles, 4½" x 8½"

5 strips, 4½" x 42"; crosscut into 36 squares, 4½" x 4½"

7 border strips, 2½" x 42"

From *each* of 13 medium or dark squares, cut:

4 squares, 4⅞" x 4⅞" (52 total)

From *each* of 35 assorted squares, cut:

1 rectangle, 4½" x 10" (35 total)
2 border strips, 2½" x 10" (70 total)

From *each* of 6 assorted squares, cut:

1 rectangle, 4½" x 10" (6 total)
1 rectangle, 2¾" x 10" (6 total)

From *each* of the 5 remaining assorted squares, cut:

2 rectangles, 4½" x 10" (10 total)

From the binding fabric, cut:

320" of 2"-wide bias binding

Making the Units

Use a scant ¼"-wide seam allowance throughout. After sewing each seam, press the seam allowances in the direction indicated by the arrows.

1. Refer to "Flying-Geese Units" on page 13. Use four matching 4⅞" medium or dark squares and one 9¼" white square to make one set of four matching flying-geese units. The units should measure 4½" x 8½". Make a total of 13 sets of four matching flying geese units (52 total).

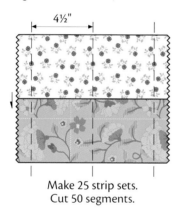

Make 52.

2. Join two 4½" x 10" rectangles along their long edges as shown (you'll have one extra rectangle). Make 25 strip sets. From each strip set, cut two 4½"-wide segments (50 total).

Make 25 strip sets.
Cut 50 segments.

3. Join two segments from step 2 (matching or different) to make a four-patch unit as shown. Repeat to make a total of 25 four-patch units, each measuring 8½" square.

Make 25.

Assembling the Quilt Top

The quilt top is assembled in rows of units, not rows of blocks. Accordingly, do not assemble the stars! And to keep the pressing easy—always press the seam allowances toward the four-patch units.

1. Lay out the flying-geese units, four-patch units, 4½" white squares, and 4½" x 8½" white rectangles in 11 rows of 11 units each as shown, making sure to use four matching flying-geese units for each star.

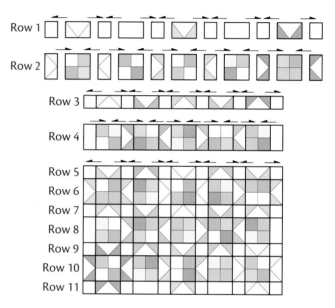

2. Sew the units together into rows. Sew the rows together to complete the quilt top. Press the seam allowances in one direction (or press them open). The quilt top should measure 64½" x 64½".

Finishing the Quilt

1. Piece the 2½"-wide inner-border strips together end to end. From the strip, cut four strips, 64½" long. Sew two inner-border strips to the sides of the quilt top and press the seam allowances toward the border.

2. Using two of the 2½" x 10" strips (matching or not), cut four 2½" squares. Sew squares to both ends of the two remaining inner-border strips and press. Sew these borders to the top and bottom of the quilt top and press the seam allowances toward the borders.

3. Sort the 68 remaining 2½" x 10" strips into two sets of 34 strips each. Join the strips in one set together as shown and press the seam allowances in one direction (or press them open). The pieced strip should measure 10" x 68½". Repeat to make a second pieced strip.

Make 2.

4. Cut each pieced strip set in half lengthwise to make a total of four outer-border strips, each measuring 5" x 68½".

5. Sew two pieced border strips to the sides of the quilt top, keeping the pinked edges on the outside. Press the seam allowances toward the outer border.

6. To make the four-patch corner units, join two 2¾" x 10" rectangles along their long edges. Make three strip sets. From the strip sets, cut eight 2¾"-wide segments. Join two segments (matching or different) to make a four-patch unit. Repeat to make a total of four corner units, each measuring 5" square.

7. Sew corner units from step 6 to both ends of the two remaining outer-border strips, keeping the pinked edges on the outside and press. Sew these borders to the top and bottom of the quilt top and press the seam allowances toward the borders.

8. Refer to page 16 for finishing your quilt, or take it to your favorite long-arm quilter for finishing. Using the 2"-wide bias binding, make and attach binding.

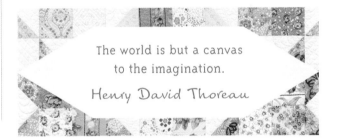

The world is but a canvas to the imagination.

Henry David Thoreau

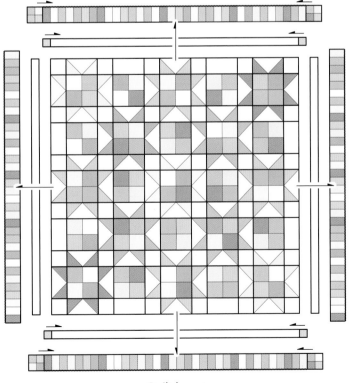

Quilt layout

PLAN C
small quilt

Pieced by Carrie Nelson. Quilted by Louise Haley.
Finished quilt size: 32½" x 32½"
Finished flying-geese-unit size: 1½" x 3"
Finished four-patch-unit size: 3" x 3"

Materials

⅝ yard of white print for block background and inner border

38 assorted 5" Charm Pack squares for blocks

31 assorted 5" Charm Pack squares for outer border

⅓ yard of fabric for binding

1¼ yards of fabric for backing

38" x 38" piece of batting

Cutting

From the white print, cut:
2 strips, 4¼" x 42"; crosscut into:
    13 squares, 4¼" x 4¼"
    8 rectangles, 2" x 3½"
2 strips, 2" x 42"; crosscut into 36 squares,
    2" x 2"
4 border strips, 1½" x 24½"

From *each* of 13 assorted squares for blocks, cut:
4 squares, 2⅜" x 2⅜" (52 total)

From *each* of 25 assorted squares for blocks, cut:
2 strips, 2" x 5" (50 total)

From *each* of 26 assorted squares for outer border, cut:

1 border strip, 1½" x 5"; trim to 3½" long (26 total)

3 border strips, 1½" x 3½" (78 total)

From *each* of 4 assorted squares for outer border, cut:

2 strips, 2" x 5" (8 total)

From the 1 remaining square for outer border, cut:

4 border squares, 1½" x 1½"

From the binding fabric, cut:

140" of 2"-wide bias binding

Making the Units

Use a scant ¼"-wide seam allowance throughout. For detailed instructions and illustrations on the following techniques refer to "Making the Units" on page 62.

1. Refer to "Flying-Geese Units" on page 13. Use four matching 2⅜" assorted squares and one 4¼" white square to make one set of four matching flying-geese units. The units should measure 2" x 3½". Make a total of 13 sets of four matching flying-geese units (52 total).

2. Sew two 2" x 5" rectangles together along their long edges to make a strip set. Make 29 strip sets. From each strip set, cut two 2"-wide segments (58 total).

3. Join two segments from step 2 (matching or different) to make a four-patch unit. Repeat to make a total of 29 four-patch units, each measuring 3½" square. Set aside four units for the outer-border corners.

Assembling and Finishing the Quilt Top

The quilt top is assembled in rows of units, not rows of blocks. Accordingly, do not assemble the stars! And to keep the pressing easy, always press the seam allowances toward the four-patch units. For detailed instructions and illustrations on the following techniques refer to "Assembling the Quilt Top" and "Finishing the Quilt Top" on pages 62 and 63.

1. Lay out the flying-geese units, four-patch units, 2" white squares, and 2" x 3½" white rectangles in 11 rows of 11 units each as shown in the photo on page 64, making sure to use four matching flying-geese units for each star.

2. Sew the units together into rows. Sew the rows together to complete the quilt top. Press the seam allowances in one direction (or press them open). The quilt top should measure 24½" x 24½".

3. Sew two 1½"-wide white inner-border strips to the sides of the quilt top and press the seam allowances toward the borders. Sew 1½" border squares to both ends of the two remaining inner-border strips, pressing the seam allowances toward the border. Sew these strips to the top and bottom of the quilt top and press the seam allowances toward the border.

4. Sort the 1½" x 3½" border strips into four sets of 26 strips each. Join the strips in one set together along their long edges and press the seam allowances in one direction (or press them open). It isn't required but try to keep all of the pinked edges on the same side! The pieced strip should measure 3½" x 26½". Repeat to make a total of four outer-border strips.

5. Sew two outer-border strips to the sides of the quilt top, keeping the pinked edges on the outside. Press the seam allowances toward the outer border.

6. Sew a remaining four-patch unit to both ends of the two remaining outer-border strips and press. Sew these borders to the top and bottom of the quilt top and press the seam allowances toward the border.

7. Refer to page 16 for finishing your quilt, or take it to your favorite long-arm quilter for finishing. Using the 2"-wide bias binding, make and attach binding.

SCRATCH

Pieced by Sue Maitre. Quilted by Diane Tricka.
Finished quilt size: 68" x 80½" • Finished Four Patch block size: 6" x 6"

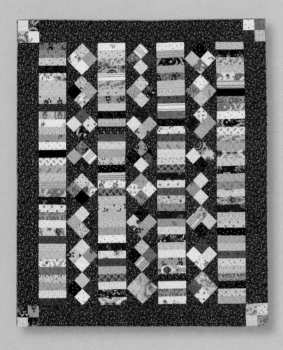

Convergence. It's when two things come together from different points. Four Patch blocks set on point and rows of Roman Coin strips met in the middle of my quilt. The Romans outnumbered the Fourps—a lovely but somewhat scrappy people—so they divided themselves up and started Boot-Scootin' Boogie-ing. What? You've never been country-western line dancing?

Name: Roman Coins—money. Scratch is a slang term for money. It was either that or Drachma. I like Scratch better too!

Materials

2⅝ yards of red print for setting triangles and border

64 assorted 10" Layer Cake squares for Four Patch blocks and Roman Coin strips

⅝ yard of fabric for binding

5 yards of fabric for backing

73" x 86" piece of batting

Cutting

From *each* of 56 assorted squares, cut:
1 strip, 3½" x 10" (56 total)
2 strips, 2½" x 10" (112 total)

From *each* of the 8 remaining assorted squares, cut:
3 strips, 2½" x 10" (24 total)

From the *lengthwise grain* of the red print, cut:
4 border strips, 6½" x 70"

7 squares, 10" x 10"; cut into quarters diagonally to yield 28 side setting triangles

From the *crosswise grain* of the remaining red print, cut:

1 strip, 10" x 42"; crosscut into 4 squares, 10" x 10". Cut the squares into quarters diagonally to yield 16 side setting triangles (2 will be extra).

1 strip, 5¼" x 42"; crosscut into 6 squares, 5¼" x 5¼". Cut the squares in half diagonally to yield 12 corner triangles.

From the binding fabric, cut:
310" of 2"-wide bias binding

Making the Four Patch Block Rows

Use a scant ¼"-wide seam allowance throughout. After sewing each seam, press the seam allowances in the direction indicated by the arrows.

1. Sew two 3½" x 10" strips together along their long edges to make a strip set. Make 28 strip sets. From each strip set, cut two 3½"-wide segments (56 total).

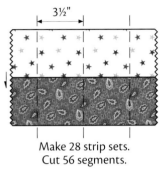

Make 28 strip sets.
Cut 56 segments.

2. Join two segments from step 1 to make a Four Patch block. Repeat to make a total of 28 Four Patch blocks, each measuring 6½" square.

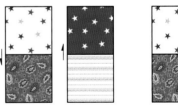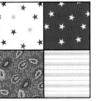

Make 28.

3. Sort the Four Patch blocks into three groups of eight blocks each. Set aside the four remaining blocks for the outer-border corners. For each Four Patch row, you'll need the following pieces:

   • Eight Four Patch blocks

   • 14 side setting triangles

   • Four corner triangles

4. Lay out the blocks and triangles as shown. The setting triangles are oversized and will be trimmed after the quilt top is assembled. Sew the pieces together into a row. Repeat to make a total of three rows.

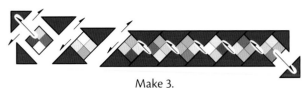

Make 3.

5. To trim and straighten the row, align the ¼" line on your long ruler with the outermost points of the blocks. Use a rotary cutter to trim any excess fabric, leaving a ¼"-wide seam allowance and making sure the corners are square. In a perfect world, after trimming, the row should measure 9" x 68½".

Making the Roman Coin Rows

1. Sort the 2½" x 10" strips into four groups of 34 strips each. Join the rectangles in one group together as shown and press the seam allowances in one direction (or press them open). The pieced row should measure 10" x 68½". Repeat to make a total of four rows.

Make 4.

2. Using a long rotary ruler, trim each rows to measure 8" wide. (If you prefer, you can join the rectangles in four segments of 8 or 9 rectangles. Press and trim the segments to 8" wide, and then join the segments together to make a finished row.)

Trim row.

Assembling and Finishing the Quilt Top

1. Lay out the Roman Coin rows and the Four Patch rows, alternating them as shown in the layout diagram. Sew the rows together, pressing the seam allowances toward the Roman Coins rows (or press them open). The quilt top should measure 56" x 68½".

2. Using the 6½"-wide border strips, trim the strips to the following lengths:

   • Side borders: two strips, 68½" long

   • Top and bottom borders: two strips, 56" long

3. Sew the side borders to the quilt top, pressing the seam allowances toward the border.

4. Sew the remaining Four Patch blocks to both ends of the two 56"-long border strips. Press the seam allowances toward the border. Sew the top and bottom borders to the quilt top and press the seam allowances toward the border.

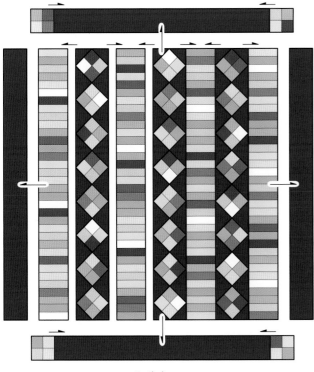

Quilt layout

5. Refer to page 16 for finishing your quilt, or take it to your favorite long-arm quilter for finishing. Using the 2"-wide bias binding, make and attach binding.

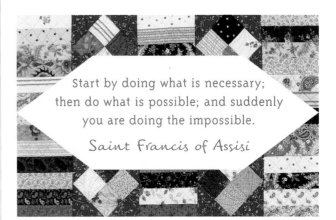

Start by doing what is necessary; then do what is possible; and suddenly you are doing the impossible.

Saint Francis of Assisi

SCRATCH
small quilt

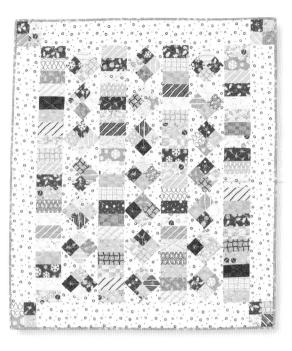

Pieced by Carrie Nelson. Quilted by Louise Haley.
Finished quilt size: 31¼" x 36½"
Finished Four Patch block size: 3" x 3"

Materials

⅞ yard of white print for setting triangles and border

65 assorted 5" Charm Pack squares for Four Patch blocks and Roman Coin strips

⅓ yard of fabric for binding

1⅓ yards of fabric for backing

37" x 42" piece of batting

Cutting

From each of the 65 assorted squares, cut:

2 strips, 2" x 5" (130 total)

From the white print, cut:

2 strips, 6¼" x 42"; crosscut into:

  9 squares, 6¼" x 6¼"; cut the squares into quarters diagonally to yield 36 side setting triangles

  6 squares, 3½" x 3½"; cut the squares in half diagonally to yield 12 corner triangles

2 border strips, 3½" x 30½"

2 border strips, 3½" x 25¼"

From the binding fabric, cut:

150" of 2"-wide bias binding

Making the Four Patch Block Rows

Use a scant ¼"-wide seam allowance throughout. For detailed instructions and illustrations on the following techniques, refer to "Making the Four Patch Block Rows" on page 68.

1. Sew two 2" x 5" strips together along their long edges to make a strip set. Make 25 strip sets. From each strip set, cut two 2"-wide segments (50 total).

2. Join two segments from step 1 to make a Four Patch unit. Repeat to make a total of 25 Four Patch blocks, each measuring 3½" square.

3. Sort the Four Patch blocks into three groups of seven blocks each. Set aside the remaining four blocks for the outer-border corners. For each Four Patch row, you'll need the following pieces:

   • Seven Four Patch blocks

   • 12 side setting triangles

   • Four corner triangles

4. Lay out the blocks and setting triangles as shown on page 68. (You will have one fewer Four Patch block in each row.) The setting triangles are oversized and will be trimmed after the quilt top is assembled. Sew the pieces together into a row. Repeat to make a total of three rows.

5. To trim and straighten the *long side edges* of each row, align the ¼" line on your long ruler with the outermost points of the blocks. Use a rotary cutter to trim any excess fabric, leaving a ¼"-wide seam allowance. In a perfect world, after trimming, the rows should measure 4¾" wide.

6. To trim and straighten the *top and bottom edges* of each row, align the ⅜" line on your long ruler with the outermost points of the blocks. Use a rotary cutter to trim any excess fabric, leaving a ⅜"-wide seam allowance. After trimming, each row must measure 30½" long to match the length of the Roman Coin rows.

Making the Roman Coin Rows

1. Sort the remaining 2" x 5" rectangles into four groups of 20 rectangles each. Join the rectangles in one group together along their long edges and press the seam allowances in one direction (or press them open). The pieced row should measure 5" x 30½". Repeat to make a total of four rows.

2. Use a long rotary ruler to trim each row to measure 3½" wide.

Assembling and Finishing the Quilt Top

For detailed instructions and illustrations on the following techniques, refer to "Assembling and Finishing the Quilt Top" on page 69.

1. Lay out the Roman Coin rows and the Four Patch rows, alternating them as shown in the photo on page 70. Sew the rows together, pressing the seam allowances toward the Roman Coins rows (or press them open). The quilt top should measure 25¼" x 30½".

2. Sew the 30½"-long border strips to the sides of the quilt top, pressing the seam allowances toward the border.

3. Sew the remaining Four Patch blocks to both ends of the two 25¼"-long border strips. Press the seam allowances toward the border. Sew the top and bottom borders to the quilt top and press the seam allowances toward the border.

4. Refer to page 16 for finishing your quilt, or take it to your favorite long-arm quilter for finishing. Using the 2"-wide bias binding, make and attach binding.

Pieced by Lisa Durst. Quilted by Cindy Paulsgrove.
Finished quilt size: 72½" x 72½" • Finished block size: 8½" x 8½"

I don't think I've ever told a story that wasn't a long one. I seem to have a propensity for turning what could be a short story into something much longer—possibly because I like using words like "propensity." Or maybe it's because I get sidetracked a lot. Whatever the reason, this quilt is a little like that. It started with an antique quilt where the only thing I liked was the block. But it had possibilities so I made a few changes—I think it's called "artistic license"—and I wound up with what you see here.

Name: I've always thought that every quilt has a story to it, whether long or short. Several years ago, I made a quilt using this block that I titled "Storyteller." Then I started playing around with charm squares and made a little quilt, which I dubbed "Short Story." And that's the end of this story.

Materials

3⅝ yards of background fabric for blocks and inner border

71 assorted 10" Layer Cake squares for blocks and outer border

⅝ yard of fabric for binding

4½ yards for backing

78" x 78" piece of batting

Omnigrid Quarter Square Triangle Ruler (98L) or Companion Angle Ruler (see note on page 74)

Cutting

From the background fabric, cut:
37 strips, 2¾" x 42"; crosscut into:
  98 rectangles, 2¾" x 10"
  98 rectangles, 2¾" x 5"
8 inner-border strips, 2¼" x 42"

From *each* of 49 assorted squares, cut:
2 strips, 2¾" x 10" (98 total)
1 strip, 2¾" x 10"; crosscut into 2 rectangles, 2¾" x 5" (98 total)

From *each* of the 22 remaining assorted squares, cut:
4 border strips, 2¼" x 10" (88 total; 6 will be extra)

From the binding fabric, cut:
300" of 2"-wide bias binding

Making the Blocks

For each block, you'll need the following pieces:

- **Background:** two 2¾" x 5" rectangles and two 2¾" x 10" rectangles

- **Assorted squares:** two 2¾" x 5" rectangles and two 2¾" x 10" rectangles (all matching)

Use a scant ¼"-wide seam allowance throughout.

1. Fold each rectangle in half and finger-crease to mark the centers as shown. With right sides together, sew 5"-long background rectangles and 10"-long assorted rectangles together, matching the center creases and aligning the edges as shown. In the same manner, sew together 5"-long assorted rectangles and 10"-long background rectangles. Press the seam allowances toward the darker rectangle. Make a total of 196 strip sets. *Note that pressing toward the darker small rectangle is easy. Pressing toward the darker large rectangle is a little more work—just make sure it is straight and that there isn't any fold at the seam line.*

2. Using one of the triangle rulers suggested below, cut a triangle from each strip set as shown. It's okay if a little "corner" is missing from the bottom of the small rectangle as long as it's within the seam allowance. Each of the rulers will show the seam line along the edge of the ruler—just check that on both sides before you cut!

- **Omnigrid Quarter Square Triangle Ruler (98L).** The top point of the ruler will extend over the top edge of the strip set, the center seam will be on the 4" line, and the bottom edge of the strip set will be on the 9" line.

- **Companion Angle Ruler.** The top of the ruler will be aligned with the edge of the fabric, the center seam will be on the 2½" line, and the bottom edge of the strip set will be on the 5" line.

Triangle Rulers

Omnigrid Quarter Square Triangle Ruler (98L) and the Companion Angle Ruler by EZ Quilting are available at most quilt shops or online.

3. Lay out four triangles from matching fabrics as shown. Sew the triangles together in pairs, taking care to match the seam intersections. Press the seam allowances toward the triangle with the darker strip on the bottom. Join the two halves, again taking care to match the seam intersections. Don't press the center seam just yet! Repeat to make a total of 49 blocks.

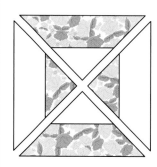 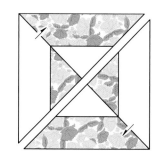

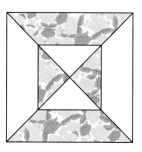

4. Use a seam ripper to remove two or three stitches from the seam allowances on *both* sides of the center seam. On the wrong side of each block, gently reposition the seam allowances to evenly distribute the fabric. Press the seam allowances in opposite directions, opening the seam so that the center lies flat. When you look at the wrong side of the block, the seam allowances should be going in a clockwise direction around the center.

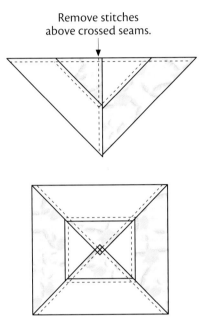

Remove stitches above crossed seams.

5. Position a 9½" (or larger) square ruler with a 45° line on top of a block, centering the 45° line along the diagonal seam line. Align the 4½" mark on the ruler with the center of the block and the 9" mark with the seam line in opposing corners as shown. Trim two sides of the block. Turn the block, realign the ruler, and trim the remaining sides. Each block should measure 9" square.

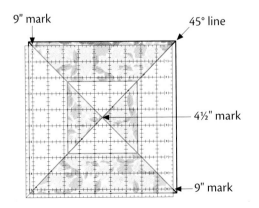

9" mark

45° line

4½" mark

9" mark

Assembling the Quilt Top

1. Lay out the blocks in seven rows of seven blocks each as shown in the quilt layout diagram on page 76.

2. Sew the blocks together into rows, pressing the seam allowances in opposite directions from one row to the next (or press them open). Then sew the rows together and press. The quilt top should measure 60" x 60".

Finishing the Quilt

1. Piece the 2¼"-wide inner-border strips together end to end. From the strip, cut four 60"-long strips. Sew two inner-border strips to the sides of the quilt top and press the seam allowances toward the border.

2. Select one 2¼" x 10" border strip and cut it into four 2¼" squares.

3. Sew squares from step 2 to both ends of the two remaining inner-border strips and press. Sew these borders to the top and bottom of the quilt top and press the seam allowances toward the border.

4. Select nine different 2¼" x 10" strips and set them aside for step 7. Divide the remaining 72 strips into two sets of 36 strips each. Join the strips in one set together as shown and press the seam allowances in one direction (or press them open). The pieced strip should measure 10" x 63½". Repeat to make a second pieced strip.

Make 2.

5. Cut each pieced strip set in half lengthwise to make a total of four outer-border strips, each measuring 5" x 63½".

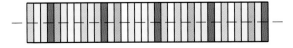

6. Sew two border strips to the sides of the quilt top, keeping the pinked edges on the outside. Press the seam allowances toward the outer border.

7. Using the remaining nine strips from step 4, trim each strip to measure 2" x 10". Sort the strips into three sets of three strips each. Join the strips in one set together along their long edges and press the seam allowances in one direction. Make three strip sets. Cut each strip set into four 2"-wide segments (12 total). Join three different segments to make a scrappy nine-patch unit for the corner square. Press the seam allowances in one direction. Make four nine-patch corner squares, each measuring 5" square.

Make 3 strip sets.
Cut 12 segments.

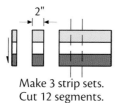

Make 4.

8. Sew nine-patch corner squares to both ends of the two remaining outer-border strips, keeping the pinked edges on the outside, and press. Sew these borders to the top and bottom of the quilt top and press the seam allowances toward the border.

9. Refer to page 16 for finishing your quilt, or take it to your favorite long-arm quilter for finishing. Using the 2"-wide bias binding, make and attach binding.

The only thing worse than being blind is having sight but no vision.

Helen Keller

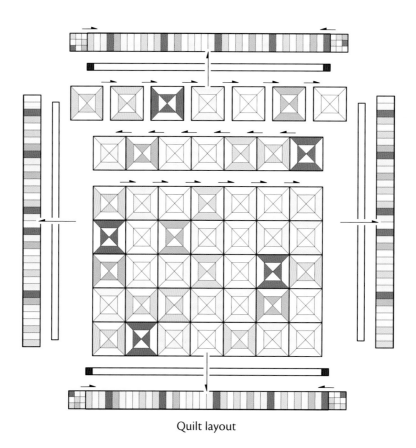

Quilt layout

SHORT STORY
small quilt

Pieced by Carrie Nelson. Quilted by Louise Haley.
Finished quilt size: 33" x 33"
Finished block size: 3¾" x 3¾"

Materials

1⅛ yards of background fabric for blocks and inner border

72 assorted Charm Pack squares for blocks and outer border

⅓ yard of fabric for binding

1⅛ yards of fabric for backing

39" x 39" piece of batting

Omnigrid Quarter Square Triangle Ruler (98L) or Companion Angle Ruler (see note on page 74)

Cutting

From the background fabric, cut:
23 strips, 1½" x 42"; crosscut into:

    4 border strips, 1½" x 26¾"

    98 rectangles, 1½" x 5"

    98 rectangles, 1½" x 2½"

From each of 49 assorted squares, cut:
2 strips, 1½" x 5" (98 total)

1 strip, 1½" x 5"; crosscut into 2 rectangles,
    1½" x 2½" (98 total)

From *each* of 22 assorted squares, cut:
3 border strips, 1½" x 5" (66 total)

From the 1 remaining square, cut;
4 border squares, 1½" x 1½"

From the binding fabric, cut:
145" of 2"-wide bias binding

Making the Blocks

For each block, you'll need the following pieces:

- **Background:** two 1½" x 2½" rectangles and two 1½" x 5" rectangles

- **Assorted squares:** two 1½" x 2½" rectangles and two 1½" x 5" rectangles, all matching

Use a scant ¼"-wide seam allowance throughout. For detailed instructions and illustrations on the following techniques refer to "Making the Blocks" on page 74.

1. In the same manner as for the larger block, fold each rectangle in half and finger-crease to mark the centers. With right sides together, sew 2½"-long background rectangles and 5"-long assorted rectangles together, matching the center creases and aligning the edges. Then sew together 2½"-long assorted rectangles and 5"-long background rectangles. Press the seam allowances toward the darker rectangle. Make a total of 196 strip sets.

2. Using one of the triangle rulers suggested below, cut a triangle from each strip set from step 1.

    - **Omnigrid Quarter Square Triangle Ruler (98L).** The top point of the ruler will extend over the top edge of the strip set, the center seam will be on the 1½" line, and the bottom edge of the strip set will be on the 4" line.

    - **Companion Angle Ruler.** The top of the ruler will be aligned with the edge of the fabric, the center seam will be on the 2½" line, and the bottom edge of the strip set will be on the 5" line.

3. Lay out four triangles from the same fabric combination. Sew the triangles together in pairs, taking care to match the seam intersections. Press the seam allowances toward the triangle with the darker strip on the bottom. Join the two halves, again taking care to match the seam intersections. Repeat to make a total of 49 blocks.

4. Position a square ruler with a 45° line on top of a block, centering the 45° line along the diagonal seam line. Align the 2⅛" mark on the ruler with the center of the block and the 4¼" mark with the seam line in opposing corners. Trim two sides of the block. Turn the block, realign the ruler, and trim the remaining sides. Each block should measure 4¼" square.

Assembling and Finishing the Quilt Top

For detailed instructions and illustrations on the following techniques refer to "Assembling the Quilt Top" and "Finishing the Quilt Top" on pages 75 and 76.

1. Lay out the blocks in seven rows of seven blocks each as shown in the photo on page 77. Sew the blocks together into rows, pressing the seam allowances in opposite directions from one row to the next (or press them open). Then sew the rows together and press. The quilt top should measure 26¾" x 26¾".

2. Sew two 1½"-wide inner-border strips to the sides of the quilt top and press the seam allowances toward the borders. Sew 1½" border squares to both ends of the two remaining 1½"-wide border strips and press. Sew these borders to the top and bottom of the quilt top and press the seam allowances toward the borders.

3. Select 56 of the 1½" x 5" border strips. Divide the strips into two sets of 28 strips. Join the strips in one set together along their long edges and press the seam allowances in one direction (or press them open). The pieced strip is about ¼" shorter than the quilt top; to adjust the length so that the border will fit properly, stitch four or five of the seams using a slightly narrower seam allowance. Measure the strip and, if necessary, adjust a few seam allowances to make the border the proper length. The border strip should measure 5" x 28¾". Repeat to make a second pieced strip.

4. Cut each pieced strip set in half lengthwise to make a total of four outer-border strips, each measuring 2½" x 28¾". Sew two border strips to the sides of the quilt top, keeping the pinked edges on the outside. Press the seam allowances toward the outer border.

5. Select six of the remaining 1½" x 5" border strips (you'll have four extra strips). Sew the strips together in pairs. Make three pairs of strips. Cut the strips into eight 1½"-wide segments. Join two different segments to make a four-patch unit for the corner squares. Make four corner squares, each measuring 2½" square.

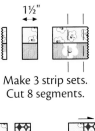

1½"

Make 3 strip sets.
Cut 8 segments.

Make 4.

6. Sew corner squares to both ends of the two remaining outer-border strips and press. Sew these borders to the top and bottom of the quilt top and press the seam allowances toward the outer border.

7. Refer to page 16 for finishing your quilt, or take it to your favorite long-arm quilter for finishing. Using the 2"-wide bias binding, make and attach binding.

SPIN CITY

Pieced by Debbie Outlaw. Quilted by Maggi Honeyman.
Finished quilt size: 72" x 72" • Finished block size: 15" x 15"

From firecrackers to amusement-park rides, I love anything that spins, twirls, or goes round-and-round. So when I find a quilt block that looks like it's spinning, it's love at first sight. This block is made entirely from strips, and you don't have to decide until the last couple of seams where you want the light and dark parts.

Name: Spin City is the name of an actual firecracker.

Materials

32 matching *pairs* of assorted 10" Layer Cake squares for blocks (64 total)

16 assorted 10" Layer Cake squares for outer border

½ yard of white print for inner border

⅝ yard of fabric for binding

4½ yards of fabric for backing

77" x 77" piece of batting

Template plastic

Permanent pen

Cutting

From *each* of the assorted squares for blocks, cut:
3 strips, 3" x 10" (6 matching strips; 192 total)

From the inner-border fabric, cut:
8 strips, 1¾" x 42"

From 1 medium or dark square for outer border, cut:
1 strip, 1¾" x 10"; crosscut into 4 squares, 1¾" x 1¾"

From *each* of the remaining 15 squares for outer border, cut:
2 border strips, 5" x 10", from the *lengthwise* grain (30 total)

From the binding fabric, cut:
300" of 2"-wide bias binding

Making the Blocks

For each block, you'll need the following pieces:

- **Fabric 1:** six matching 3" x 10" strips

- **Fabric 2:** six matching 3" x 10" strips

Use a scant ¼"-wide seam allowance throughout. Directions are for making one block. Repeat to make a total of 16 blocks. After sewing each seam, press the seam allowances in the direction indicated by the arrows.

1. From the template plastic, cut a 3" x 10" rectangle. On the right side of the template, use a permanent pen to mark a point 3½" from the top as shown. On the left side of the template, mark a point 6½" from the top. Draw a diagonal line connecting the two points. *The template must look exactly like the one shown in the diagram.* Using a rotary cutter and ruler, cut the rectangle apart on the drawn line to make a cutting-guide template.

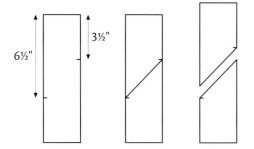

2. Use a piece of clear tape to affix the template to the underneath side of a small ruler with the diagonal edge of the template along the outer edge of the ruler as shown above right. This template is used as a guide only to make trimming the strips easier.

3. Using the template/ruler and two 3" x 10" strips of each fabric, trim the strips exactly as shown. *If you have stacked your strips, make sure that all of the strips are right side facing up before cutting!* It's important that the pieces match the diagram or you'll need more Layer Cake squares.

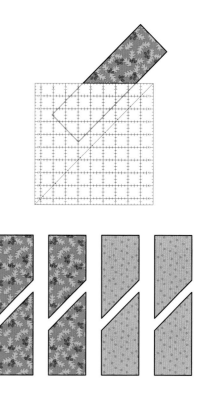

4. Join two pieces from step 3 to make a strip, offsetting the ends as shown. Again, the pieced strip must match the diagram. Press the seam allowances open. Repeat to make four matching pieced strips.

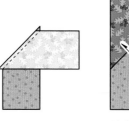

Make 4.

5. Trim the pieced strips to measure 3" x 8". After trimming, the seam line on the right edge should be 2½" from the top and the seam on the left edge should be 5½" from the top as shown. Trim the eight remaining strips (four of each fabric) to measure 3" x 8".

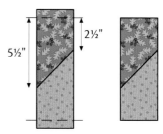

6. Lay out three strips side by side, placing the pieced strip in the center as shown. Sew the strips together. Make four matching units.

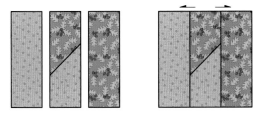

Make 4.

7. Lay out the units in a four-patch arrangement, rotating the units as shown. Before stitching, lay out the same units in reverse order. Which way do you prefer? (I like to vary the placement of the light and dark fabrics so that not all of the blocks have a light background.)

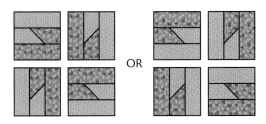

OR

8. Sew the pieces together in rows, and then sew the rows together to complete a block, taking care to match the seam intersection in the center of the block. Don't press the center seam just yet. Repeat to make a total of 16 blocks.

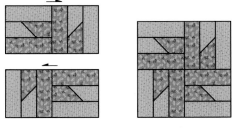

Make 16.

9. Use a seam ripper to remove two or three stitches from the seam allowances on *both* sides of the center seam, as shown. On the wrong side of each block, gently reposition the seam allowances to evenly distribute the fabric. Press the seam

allowances in opposite directions, opening the seam so that the center lies flat. When you look at the wrong side of the block, the seam allowances should be going in a counterclockwise direction around the center. Each block should measure 15½" square.

Remove stitching above crossed seams.

Assembling the Quilt Top

1. Lay out the blocks in four rows of four blocks each as shown in the quilt layout diagram.

2. Sew the blocks together into rows, pressing the seam allowances in opposite directions from one row to the next (or press them open). Then sew the rows together and press. The quilt top should measure 60½" x 60½".

Finishing the Quilt Top

1. Piece the 1¾"-wide inner-border strips together end to end. From the strip, cut four strips 60½" long. Sew two inner-border strips to the sides of the quilt top and press the seam allowances toward the border.

2. Sew a 1¾" square to both ends of the two remaining inner-border strips and press. Sew these borders to the top and bottom of the quilt top and press the seam allowances toward the border.

3. For the outer border, sort the 5" x 10" border strips into the following groups:

• **Side borders:** two groups of seven strips each

• **Top and bottom borders:** two groups of eight strips each

Join each group of strips end to end to make four long strips. Press the seam allowances in one direction (or press them open). For the side borders, trim the two shorter strips to measure 5" x 63". For the top and bottom borders, trim the two longer strips to measure 5" x 72".

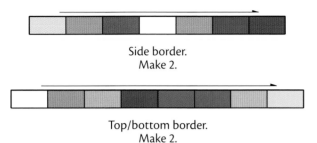

Side border.
Make 2.

Top/bottom border.
Make 2.

4. Sew the border strips to the sides, and then the top and bottom of the quilt top as shown in the layout diagram, keeping the pinked edges on the outside. Press the seam allowances toward the outer borders.

5. Refer to page 16 for finishing your quilt, or take it to your favorite long-arm quilter for finishing. Using the 2"-wide bias binding, make and attach binding.

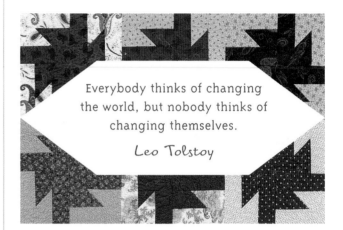

Everybody thinks of changing the world, but nobody thinks of changing themselves.

Leo Tolstoy

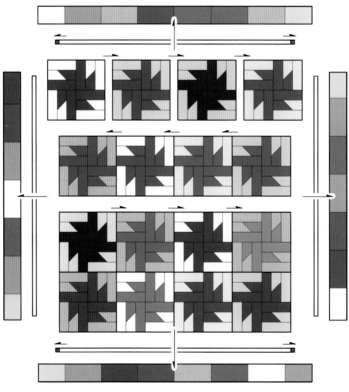

Quilt layout

Spin City
small quilt

Pieced by Carrie Nelson. Quilted by Louise Haley.
Finished quilt size: 30½" x 30½"
Finished block size: 6" x 6"

Materials

32 matching *pairs* of assorted 5" Charm Pack squares for blocks (64 total)

14 assorted 5" Charm Pack squares for outer border

¼ yard of white print for inner border

⅓ yard of fabric for binding

1⅛ yards of fabric for backing

36" x 36" piece of batting

Template plastic

Permanent pen

Cutting

From *each* of the assorted squares for blocks, cut:
3 strips, 1½" x 5" (6 matching strips; 192 total)

From the inner-border fabric, cut:
4 strips, 1½" x 24½"

From 1 square for outer border, cut:
4 squares, 1½" x 1½"

From *each* of the remaining 13 assorted

squares for outer border, cut:
2 border strips, 2½" x 5" (26 total; don't worry about
the pinked edges)

From the binding fabric, cut:
135" of 2"-wide bias binding

Making the Blocks

For each block, you'll need the following pieces:

- Fabric 1: six matching 1½" x 5" strips

- Fabric 2: six matching 1½" x 5" strips

Use a scant ¼"-wide seam allowance throughout.
Directions are for making one block. Repeat to
make a total of 16 blocks. For detailed instructions
and illustrations on the following techniques refer to
"Making the Blocks" on page 82.

1. From the template plastic, cut a 1½" x 5"
   rectangle. On the right side of the template, mark
   a point 1¾" from the top. On the left side of the
   template, mark a point 3¼" from the top. Draw
   a diagonal line connecting the two points. Cut
   the rectangle apart on the drawn line to make a
   cutting-guide template.

2. Use a piece of clear tape to affix the template
   to the underneath side of a small ruler with the
   template's diagonal edge along the outer edge
   of the ruler. Using the template/ruler and two
   1½" x 5" strips of each fabric, trim the strips
   exactly as shown in step 3 on page 82, making
   sure all of the strips are right side facing up before
   cutting.

3. Using two different pieces from step 2, sew the
   pieces together to make a strip. Press the seam
   allowances open. Repeat to make four matching
   pieced strips.

4. Trim the pieced strips to measure 1½" x 3½". After
   trimming, the seam line on the right edge should
   be 1" from the top and the seam on the left edge
   should be 2½" from the top as shown. Trim the
   eight remaining strips (four of each fabric)
   to measure 1½" x 3½".

5. Lay out three strips side by side, placing the
   pieced strip in the center as shown in step 6 on
   page 83. Sew the strips together. Make four
   matching units.

6. Lay out the units in a four-patch arrangement,
   rotating the units in the same manner as the
   larger block. Sew the pieces together in rows and
   then sew the rows together to complete a block.
   Repeat to make a total of 16 blocks.

Assembling and Finishing the Quilt Top

For detailed instructions and illustrations on the
following techniques refer to "Assembling the Quilt
Top" and "Finishing the Quilt Top" on pages 83
and 84.

1. Lay out the blocks in four rows of four blocks
   each as shown in the photo on page 85. Sew
   the blocks together into rows, pressing the seam
   allowances in opposite directions from one row to
   the next (or press them open). Then sew the rows
   together and press. The quilt top should measure
   24½" x 24½".

2. Sew two 1½"-wide inner-border strips to the sides
   of the quilt top and press the seam allowances
   toward the borders.

3. Sew a 1½" square to both ends of the two
   remaining inner-border strips and press. Sew these
   borders to the top and bottom of the quilt top and
   press the seam allowances toward the borders.

4. For the outer border, sort 2½" x 5" border strips into the following groups:

   • **Side borders:** two groups of six strips each

   • **Top and bottom borders:** two groups of seven strips each

Join each group of strips end to end to make four long strips. Press the seam allowances in one direction (or press them open). For the side borders, trim the two shorter strips to measure 2½" x 26½". For the top and bottom borders, trim the two longer strips to measure 2½" x 30½".

5. Sew the border strips to the sides, and then the top and bottom of the quilt top, keeping the pinked edges on the outside. Press the seam allowances toward the outer borders.

6. Refer to page 16 for finishing your quilt, or take it to your favorite long-arm quilter for finishing. Using the 2"-wide bias binding, make and attach binding.

Pieced by Sue Maitre. Quilted by Diane Tricka.
Finished quilt size: 69" x 69"

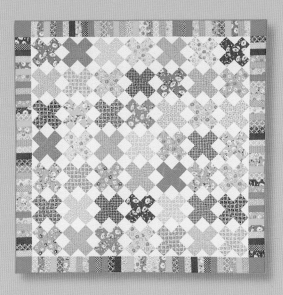

Can I tell you a secret? *This is my favorite quilt in this book. Shhhh!* I know, I'm not supposed to have a favorite quilt so just never you mind what I wrote in the introduction to "Bennington." I'll just call this one my "love child" because it looks good in every fabric, it's fun to make, and I keep picking fabrics so that I can make another one. After all, there are so many beautiful Layer Cakes available—and this quilt doesn't take that long to make—I'm sorry. I got a little sidetracked there. What? Oh, you want to know why I love this quilt so much. That's easy: all you have to do is cut out the pieces, lay them out, and start sewing. Add a little bit of chocolate and it's the perfect way to spend a day.

Name: What else can you call a quilt with all those little Xs? Tic-Tac-Toe? X Marks the Spot? Sue came up with this one and when my mom said it was her favorite from all the options, that sealed the deal.

Materials

1¾ yards of background fabric for squares and setting triangles

49 assorted 10" Layer Cake squares for squares and rectangles

18 assorted 10" Layer Cake squares for border

⅝ yard of fabric for binding

4½ yards of fabric for backing

74" x 74" piece of batting

Cutting

From the background fabric, cut:

11 strips, 3½" x 42"; crosscut into 120 squares, 3½" x 3½"

3 strips, 5¾" x 42"; crosscut into:

13 squares, 5¾" x 5¾"; cut into quarters diagonally to yield 52 side setting triangles

2 squares, 3¼" x 3¼"; cut in half diagonally to yield 4 corner triangles

From *each* of the 49 assorted squares, cut:

2 strips, 3½" x 10"; crosscut into:

1 rectangle, 3½" x 9½" (49 total)

2 squares, 3½" x 3½" (98 total)

From *each* of 17 assorted squares for border, cut:

4 border strips, 2¼" x 10" (68 total)

From the 1 remaining square for border, cut:

4 border squares, 5" x 5"

From the binding fabric, cut:

290" of 2"-wide bias binding

Assembling the Quilt Top

Use a scant ¼"-wide seam allowance throughout. After sewing each seam, press the seam allowances in the direction indicated by the arrows.

1. On a design wall or large flat surface, arrange the 3½" background squares and the assorted squares and rectangles as shown; be sure to keep matching pieces together so that they will form an X. Place the setting triangles around the outer edges, and then add the corner triangles. The triangles are oversized and will be trimmed after the quilt top is assembled.

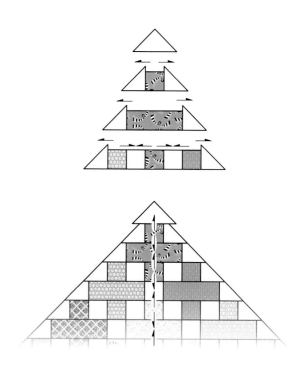

2. Once you are satisfied with the arrangement, start in one corner and sew the pieces together into rows. Sew the rows together, matching the seam intersections.

Finishing the Quilt

1. To trim and straighten the quilt top, align the ¼" line on your long ruler with the outermost points of the Xs. Use a rotary cutter to trim any excess fabric, leaving a ¼"-wide seam allowance, making sure the corners are square. The quilt top should measure 60" x 60".

Skosh More Room

I prefer to trim the seam allowance to ⅜". It gives me a little bit of leeway in case one X sticks out a skosh more than its neighbors. The larger seam allowance also makes it easier for me to attach my pieced border and press it without chopping off a couple of corners. Even though this is an X-rated quilt, the fit doesn't have to be too tight.

2. Divide the 2¼" x 10" strips into two sets of 34 strips each. Join the strips in one set together as shown and press the seam allowances in one direction (or press them open). The pieced strip should measure 10" x 60". Repeat to make a second pieced strip.

Make 2.

3. Cut each pieced strip set in half lengthwise to make a total of four outer-border strips, each measuring 5" x 60".

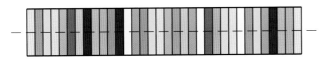

4. Sew two outer-border strips to the sides of the quilt top, keeping the pinked edges on the outside. Press the seam allowances toward the outer border.

5. Sew a 5" border square to both ends of the two remaining border strips, keeping the pinked edges on the outside, and press. Sew these borders to the top and bottom of the quilt top and press the seam allowances toward the borders.

6. Refer to page 16 for finishing your quilt, or take it to your favorite long-arm quilter for finishing. Using the 2"-wide bias binding, make and attach binding.

The drawback to a journey that has been too well planned is that it does not leave enough room for adventure.

André Gide

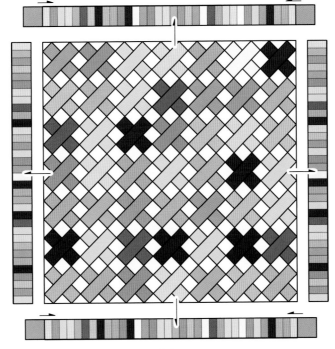

Quilt layout

X-RATED
small quilt

Pieced by Carrie Nelson. Quilted by Louise Haley.
Finished quilt size: 30" x 30"

Materials

⅝ yard of background fabric for squares and setting triangles

36 assorted 5" Charm Pack squares for squares and rectangles

18 assorted 5" Charm Pack squares for border

⅓ yard of fabric for binding

1⅛ yards of fabric for backing

35" x 35" piece of batting

Cutting

From the background fabric, cut:

5 strips, 2" x 42"; crosscut into 85 squares, 2" x 2"

2 strips, 4" x 42" crosscut into:

11 squares, 4" x 4"; cut into quarters diagonally to yield 44 side setting triangles

2 squares, 3" x 3"; cut in half diagonally to yield 4 corner triangles

From *each* of the 36 assorted squares, cut:

1 strip, 2" x 5"; crosscut into 2 squares, 2" x 2" (72 total)

1 strip, 2" x 5" (36 total)

From *each* of 17 assorted squares for border, cut:
2 border strips, 2" x 5" (34 total)

From the 1 remaining square for border, cut:
4 border squares, 2½" x 2½"

From the binding fabric, cut:
130" of 2"-wide bias binding

Assembling and Finishing the Quilt Top

As easy as the big one is, this one is easier. It's smaller and the seams are shorter. Use a scant ¼"-wide seam allowance throughout. For detailed instructions and illustrations on the following techniques refer to "Assembling the Quilt Top" and "Finishing the Quilt Top" on pages 90 and 91.

1. On a design wall or large flat surface, arrange the 2" background squares and the assorted squares and rectangles as shown in the photo; be sure to keep the matching pieces together so that they will form an X. Place the setting triangles around the outer edges, and then add the corner triangles. The triangles are oversized and will be trimmed after the quilt top is assembled.

2. Once you're satisfied with the arrangement, start in one corner and sew the pieces together into rows, pressing the seam allowances toward the background pieces. Sew the rows together, matching the seam intersection, and press the seam allowances in one direction.

3. To trim and straighten the quilt top, align the ¼" line on your long ruler with the outermost points of the Xs. Use a rotary cutter to trim any excess fabric, leaving a ¼"-wide seam allowance and making sure the corners are square. The quilt top should measure 26" x 26".

4. Divide the 2" x 5" border strips into two sets of 17 strips each. Join the strips in one set together along their long edges and press the seam allowances in one direction (or press them open). The pieced strip should measure 5" x 26". Repeat to make a second pieced strip.

5. Cut each pieced strip set in half lengthwise to make a total of four outer-border strips, each measuring 2½" x 26".

6. Sew two outer-border strips to the sides of the quilt top, keeping the pinked edges on the outside. Press the seam allowances toward the border.

7. Sew a 2½" border square to both ends of the two remaining border strips, keeping the pinked edges on the outside, and press. Sew these borders to the top and bottom of the quilt top and press the seam allowances toward the border.

8. Refer to page 16 for finishing your quilt, or take it to your favorite long-arm quilter for finishing. Using the 2"-wide bias binding, make and attach binding.

Acknowledgments

Not so long ago, someone asked me about my staff. Huh? Staff? It's just me. No office girls, no girl Friday, no right-hand man—except that that isn't the whole story. I owe a lot of people a debt of gratitude that I doubt I can ever come close to repaying, but I'm sure going to try. So here goes.

Lisa Durst, Nicole Reed, Darlene Johannis, Mary Dyer, Marsha Heberlein, Sue Maitre, Judy Adams, Debbie Outlaw, and Lissa Alexander—there isn't any way that I could have gotten everything done on time without you. As busy as you all were, you still jumped in and worked overtime to make me look good. Thank you hardly seems adequate.

Diane Tricka, Louise Haley, Darlene Johannis, Maggi Honeyman, Cindy Pelligrini, Paula Cosgrove, and Debbie Thornton—it isn't a quilt until it's quilted. Thank you for working your magic, and for working it so quickly.

A special thank-you to Diane and Louise—you do the majority of my quilts and I wish you could be there when your beautiful work is admired by the glitterati of the quilting world. I feel very privileged to be on your client list.

Moda Lissa—thank you for thinking of me when you get an idea. As always, you were right and this was definitely a lot of fun. And thank you for the fabric!

My friends Ginger Sanchez, Sue Maitre, and Judy Adams—thank you for listening to me whine and kvetch about one thing and another, and for pushing me along when I get bogged down. You're always there with good advice and a level head.

Thank you Mom for packing so many patterns and for thinking all my quilts are beautiful…even the ones that aren't.

And, finally, Karen, Mary, Cathy, Nancy, Sheila, and all the wonderful folks at Martingale & Company—I know I was really late, so I can't thank you enough for waiting around for me to get to the party! I would have been there sooner but Rosie ate my watch.

ABOUT ROSIE

Or, everything you've ever wanted to know about the real star of the show.

Just in case you don't already know this about Miss Rosie's Quilt Co., my name is Carrie and Rosie is my golden retriever. She has top billing because she's prettier, nicer, and she used to be younger than I am. You would think I'd have more power because I do the math for our little business, but you'd be wrong. A cold wet nose is a pretty powerful weapon when it comes to getting your way.

At 10 years old, Rosie is a little bit less dignified than she'd like you to believe she is. A quilt isn't really a quilt until she's rolled around and slept on it. She still inspects every bag, box, and package that comes into the house, especially those boxes of fabric from Moda since they're addressed to her anyway. And, yes, she really did eat a watch. And a few years ago, she swallowed a package of needles…but that's a story for another time.

While Rosie isn't much of a quilter, she's an excellent quilting teacher. Her "golden rules" are simple: Play every day and enjoy it to the fullest. Jump into everything with unabashed enthusiasm and a passion for what you're doing. Don't worry about what anybody else thinks; as long as you're happy and having fun, that truly is the only thing that matters. And no matter what, always be open to new adventures, new ideas, and new challenges.

Pretty and smart! No wonder it's her name on the company logo.

There's More Online!

- See more of Carrie's quilts, explore her other books and patterns, and check out her teaching schedule at www.missrosiesquiltco.com

- Read Carrie's blog at http://lavieenrosie.typepad.com

- Find more terrific books on quilting, knitting, crochet, and more at www.martingale-pub.com

MISS ROSIE'S QUILT Co.

You might also enjoy these other fine titles from Martingale & Company

Study the alphabet and number chart.
Then trace the letters and numbers.

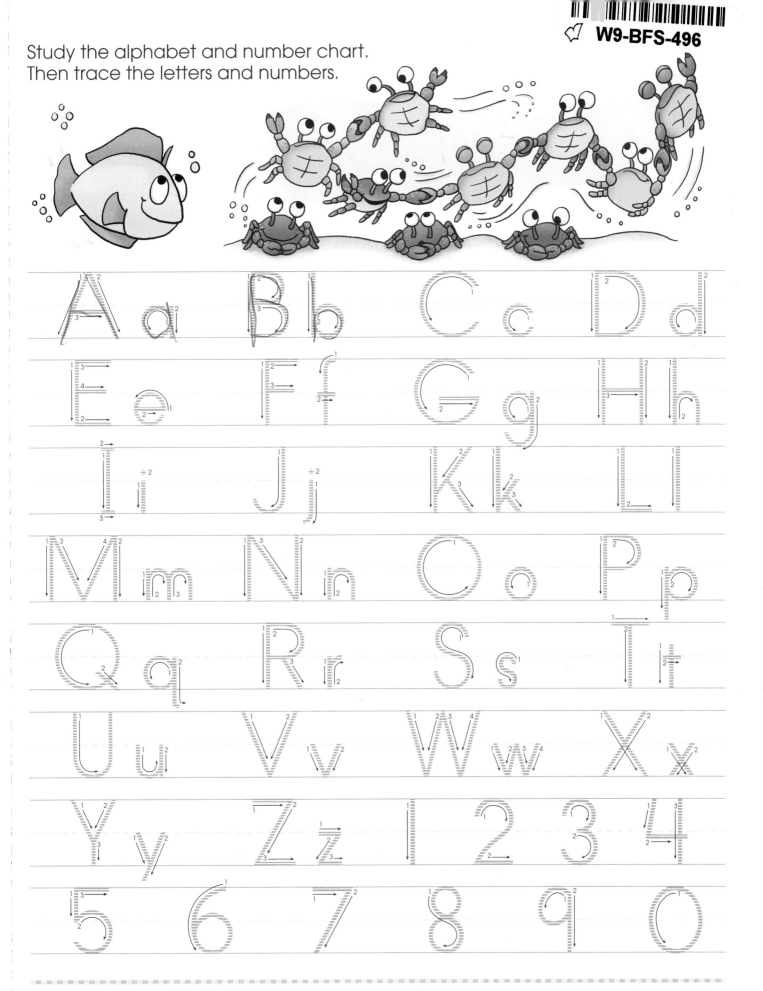

Manuscript Writing

Look at the arrows. Trace each letter.
Now write the letters and words.

A A A A A A
A A A A A

a a a a a a a
a a a a a
a a a a a a a

Annie Annie Annie
Annie Annie Annie

ant ant ant ant ant
ant ant ant ant

Manuscript Writing

Fun with A

Read the riddle.
Write the answer you think is funny.

How many months have 28 days?

all of them	none of them

the funny one is all of them.

What is smaller than an ant's mouth?

an ant's dinner	an ant's leg

The funny one is an ants

dinner.

Look at the arrows. Trace each letter.
Now write the letters and words.

B B B B B B

B B B B B B

B B B B B B

b b b b b b b

b b b b b b b b

b b b b b b b b b b

Billy Billy Billy Billy

Billy Billy Billy

bear bear bear bear

bear bear bear

4

Manuscript Writing

Fun with B

Read the riddle.
Write the answer you think is funny.

What do you call a baby insect?

(a baby buggy)	a bug

the funny one is a
baby buggy.

What is a sleeping bull?

a sleepy bull	(a bull dozer)

the funny one is a
bull dozer,

Look at the arrows. Trace each letter.
Now write the letters and words.

C C C C C

C C C C C C

C C C C C C C C C C

C C C C C C C C C C C

C C C C C C C C C C

C C C C C C C C C C

Casey Casey Casey

Casey casey casey

cat cat cat cat

cat cat cat

Fun with C

Read the riddle.
Write the answer you think is funny.

What has two hands but no arms?

| a clown | a clock |

the funny one is a

clown

What kind of person likes cocoa?

| a coconut | a nut |

a nut

Look at the arrows. Trace each letter.
Now write the letters and words.

D D D   D D D

D D   D D D D

D D   D D   D D

d d   d d d d d   d d

d d d   d d d   d d d d

d d d   d d   d d   d d

David   David David

David   David

duck   duck duck duck

duck   duck

8

Manuscript Writing

Fun with D

Read the riddle.
Write the answer you think is funny.

What kind of nut has no shell?

| a doughnut | a peanut |

A doughnut

Where can you always find money?

| in your pocket | in the dictionary |

In the dictionary.

Ohcomasta

Look at the arrows. Trace each letter.
Now write the letters and words.

E E E E E

E E E E E E

E E E E E E E

e e e e e e e e

e e e e e e

Elmer

elf

Fun with E

Read the riddle.
Write the answer you think is funny.

What is the biggest ant?

a red ant	an elephant

a red ant

What three letter word sounds like one letter?

eye	pie

SPY

Look at the arrows. Trace each letter.
Now write the letters and words.

F F

f f

Fran

fox

Fun with F

Read the riddle.
Write the answer you think is funny.

What keeps football players cool?

their fans	ice cubes

Ice

What does a snowman eat for dinner?

pizza	frozen dinners

Look at the arrows. Trace each letter.
Now write the letters and words.

G G

g g

Gary

goat

Fun with G

Read the riddle.
Write the answer you think is funny.

What kind of cookie must be handled carefully?

| a sugar cookie | a ginger snap |

_____

_____

_____

_____

Which bug can tell fortunes?

| a gypsy moth | a butterfly |

_____

_____

_____

_____

Look at the arrows. Trace each letter.
Now write the letters and words.

Harry

horse

Fun with H

Read the riddle.
Write the answer you think is funny.

What did the bee say to the flower?

| Hello, honey. | Hello, pretty. |

_____

_____

_____

_____

Who always goes to bed with his shoes on?

| my dad | a horse |

_____

_____

_____

_____

Look at the arrows. Trace each letter.
Now write the letters and words.

2→
1
↓
3→
I

2
1
↓
i

Ike

iguana

Fun with I

Read the riddle.
Write the answer you think is funny.

What person has the loudest voice?

| my mother | the ice cream man |

Where do fish sleep?

| in a river bed | in a bunk bed |

Look at the arrows. Trace each letter.
Now write the letters and words.

J J

j j

Jason

jay

Fun with J

Read the riddle.
Write the answer you think is funny.

What kind of bird is like a letter?

| a jaybird | an owl |

What beans are not in a garden?

| green beans | jelly beans |

Look at the arrows. Trace each letter.
Now write the letters and words.

K K

k k

Kelly

koala

Fun with K

Read the riddle.
Write the answer you think is funny.

Where do children grow?

| in kindergarten | in a flower garden |

What letter is like a girl's name?

| the letter R | the letter K |

HELLO,
MY NAME
IS

Look at the arrows. Trace each letter.
Now write the letters and words.

Leon

lion

Fun with L

Read the riddle.
Write the answer you think is funny.

How should you treat a baby goat?

like your sister	like a kid

What time is the best time to catch a frog?

leap year	spring

Look at the arrows. Trace each letter.
Now write the letters and words.

M M M

m m m

Mandy

mouse

Fun with M

Read the riddle.
Write the answer you think is funny.

Who always eats the most at a picnic?

mosquitoes	the dog

_____

_____

_____

_____

What star is famous?

an old star	a movie star

_____

_____

_____

_____

Look at the arrows. Trace each letter.
Now write the letters and words.

N N

n n

Nina

newt

Fun with N

Read the riddle.
Write the answer you think is funny.

How do you catch a squirrel?

climb a tree	act like a nut

_____

_____

_____

_____

Who makes up jokes about knitting?

a nitwit	kids

_____

_____

_____

_____

Look at the arrows. Trace each letter.
Now write the letters and words.

O O

o o

Omar

owl

Fun with O

What kind of cat lives in the ocean?

| an octopus | a fat cat |

What would you call a grandfather clock?

| an old clock | an old timer |

Look at the arrows. Trace each letter.
Now write the letters and words.

P P

p p

Peter

panda

Fun with P

Read the riddle.
Write the answer you think is funny.

How do pigs write?

with a pencil	with a pigpen

What lands on its head as often as its tail?

a penny	a dog

Look at the arrows. Trace each letter.
Now write the letters and words.

Q Q

q q

Quincy

quail

Fun with Q

Read the riddle.
Write the answer you think is funny.

What food does a duck like best?

quackers	popcorn

_____

_____

_____

_____

Why is the moon like a dollar?

It has cents.	It has four quarters.

_____

_____

_____

_____

Look at the arrows. Trace each letter.
Now write the letters and words.

R R

r r

Rich

rabbit

Fun with R

Read the riddle.
Write the answer you think is funny.

What runs but cannot walk?

a river	a duck

What piece of wood is like a king?

a yardstick	a ruler

Look at the arrows. Trace each letter.
Now write the letters and words.

S S

s s

Sally

seal

Fun with S

Read the riddle.
Write the answer you think is funny.

What is never out of sight?

| the letter s | the sun |

What fish is famous?

| a goldfish | a starfish |

Look at the arrows. Trace each letter.
Now write the letters and words.

T T T

t t t

Tony

turtle

Fun with T

Read the riddle.
Write the answer you think is funny.

Who had the first mobile home?

| a cow | a turtle |

How many worms make a foot?

| twelve inchworms | ten inchworms |

Manuscript Writing

Look at the arrows. Trace each letter.
Now write the letters and words.

U U U

u u u

Ursula

unicorn

Fun with U

Read the riddle.
Write the answer you think is funny.

What can be a cane or a tent?

| an umbrella | a tree |

What never goes down?

| in | up |

Look at the arrows. Trace each letter.
Now write the letters and words.

V v

V v

Vicky

vulture

Fun with V

Read the riddle.
Write the answer you think is funny.

Where do old Volkswagens go?

| the junkyard | the old Volks home |

Who would rob a blood bank?

| a vampire | a robin |

Look at the arrows. Trace each letter.
Now write the letters and words.

W w

W w

Wendy

wolf

Fun with W

Read the riddle.
Write the answer you think is funny.

What kind of dog keeps time?

| a watchdog | a big dog |

How did the ocean say goodbye?

| It roared. | It waved. |

Look at the arrows. Trace each letter.
Now write the letters and words.

X X X

X X X

Xavier

x-ray

Fun with X

Read the riddle.
Write the answer you think is funny.

What can see right through you?

your mother	an x-ray

What phone can't you use to call home?

a xylophone	a pink phone

Look at the arrows. Trace each letter.
Now write the letters and words.

Y Y

y y

Yancy

yak

Fun with Y

Read the riddle.
Write the answer you think is funny.

What is never out of you?

the letter y	the letter c

What animal talks a lot?

a fish	a yak

Manuscript Writing

Look at the arrows. Trace each letter.
Now write the letters and words.

Z Z Z

Z Z Z

Zack

zebra

Fun with Z

Read the riddle.
Write the answer you think is funny.

What is black and white and red all over?

| a horse | a sunburned zebra |

What has teeth but does not bite?

| a zipper | a dog |

Trace and write.

Monday

Tuesday

Wednesday

Thursday

Monday
Go to park

Tuesday
School Concert

Wednesday
Cleanup room

Friday

Saturday

Sunday

Thursday
Soccer Practice

Friday
Go to library

Saturday
Beach Day

Sunday
Picnic

Trace and write. Use the extra lines to practice.

January

February

March

April

May

June

57

Trace and write. Use the extra lines to practice.

July

August

September

October

November

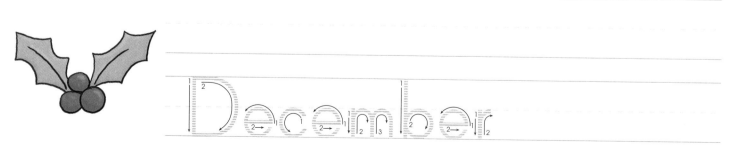

December

Trace and write the color word.
Color the picture.

Color the 🍎 red.

red

Color the 🍊 orange.

orange

Color the 🍌 yellow.

yellow

Color the 🍃 green.

green

Color the 🫐 blue.

blue

Color the 🟣🟣 purple.

purple

Color the 🥥 brown.

brown

Fill in the missing letters.

Fill in the missing letters.

Manuscript Writing

Trace and write.

1 one

2 two

3 three

4 four

5 five

6 six

7 seven

8 eight

9 nine

10 ten

Manuscript Writing 02251